ChatGPT for Beginners: Mastering AI Conversations

Unlock the Potential of ChatGPT and Learn How It Can Make Your Life Easier, Simpler, and Richer

Malcolm Oppenheimer

© **Copyright 2023 - All rights reserved.**

The content contained within this book may not be reproduced, duplicated or transmitted without direct written permission from the author or the publisher.

Under no circumstances will any blame or legal responsibility be held against the publisher, or author, for any damages, reparation, or monetary loss due to the information contained within this book, either directly or indirectly.

Legal Notice:

This book is copyright protected. It is only for personal use. You cannot amend, distribute, sell, use, quote or paraphrase any part, or the content within this book, without the consent of the author or publisher.

Disclaimer Notice:

Please note the information contained within this document is for educational and entertainment purposes only. All effort has been executed to present accurate, up to date, reliable, complete information. No warranties of any kind are declared or implied. Readers acknowledge that the author is not engaged in the rendering of legal, financial, medical or professional advice. The content within this book has been derived from various sources. Please consult a licensed professional before attempting any techniques outlined in this book.

By reading this document, the reader agrees that under no circumstances is the author responsible for any losses, direct or indirect, that are incurred as a result of the use of the information contained within this document, including, but not limited to, errors, omissions, or inaccuracies.

Contents

Introduction	5
1. WHEN BOTS START TALKING BACK	9
Back to the AI Stone Age	10
Decoding the Jargon: AI Characteristics	26
OpenAI and Its Language Model, GPT-4	33
2. THROUGH THE LOOKING GLASS	39
Architecture and Functioning of ChatGPT	40
Prompt Engineering	51
No AI Is Perfect	57
3. YOUR PERSONAL BUTLER	63
Becoming the Butler	64
Prompts to Use for ChatGPT	79
4. THERAPY ON DEMAND	85
Mind Matters	86
Can AI Really Care?	93
Let's Talk It Out	97
Prompts to Use for Your Therapist on Demand	100
5. YOUR POCKET-SIZED BUSINESS PARTNER	103
Redefining Business Communication	104
The Wordsmith	112
The Silent Analyst	121
The Unsleeping Customer Rep	130
The Digital Marketer	140
Prompts for Your Pocket-sized Business Partner	148
6. A NEW ROOMMATE, BUT LESS NOISY	153
Your AI Roommate	154
Safeguarding Your Space	160

7. PUSHING CHATGPT TO ITS (MILDLY SARCASTIC) LIMIT	171
Power Tools	171
The Art of the Impossible	187
8. WOOING WORDS FROM YOUR WITTY AI	193
A Linguist's Playground	194
ChatGPT and Accessibility	204
Afterword	209
Glossary	213
References	215

Introduction

Welcome, my soon-to-be tech savvy reader, to your cheat sheet for succeeding in the digital world. Technology has infiltrated almost every aspect of our lives, and will only continue to do so. Whether this is a good thing or a bad depends on your point of view, and how well-placed you are to use said tech to improve the brief time you have on this mortal coil.

Over the past few decades, computational devices have taken the world by storm, helping us to do more, learn more, and achieve more than ever before. The average person now has access to technology that, a few hundred years ago, was only considered a possibility by science fiction writers. During the time between then and now, there have been a few revolutionary inventions that have changed the very fabric of our existence. These include the likes of the personal computer, the internet, the phone, and most recently, conversational artificial intelligence (AI). At the forefront of this latest technological revolution is a deep learning, large language model called ChatGPT (chat generative pre-trained transformer).

Within two months of its launch on November 30, 2022, the generative chatbot developed by OpenAI had already reached 100 million monthly users, and this number has only continued to grow. To put it into perspective, it took TikTok nine whole months to reach the 100 million mark, while it took Instagram a whopping two-and-a-half years to achieve this same milestone. This makes ChatGPT the "fastest-growing consumer application in history" (Hu, 2023).

Despite its ever-increasing popularity, there has been some hesitation and resistance towards this groundbreaking new technology. These fears center around concerns about data security and privacy, as well as the platform's potential misuse by nefarious individuals; and the biggest worry of them all, that ChatGPT will mean the further loss of jobs for us humans. While it can often feel like we are drowning in a sea of ever-increasing technological complexity, I'm here to tell you it is possible to ride the techno-wave, using the tools at our disposal to make our lives better and our futures brighter, without the risk of losing our lunch to it. All it takes is learning to use it right, which lucky for you, is exactly what this book is here to teach you!

In the pages and chapters to follow, we're going to break down this revolutionary new technology bit by bit, step by step, as we discover the vast array of ways that ChatGPT can help to transform your life. We'll begin our journey into the world of generative chatbots way back in the Stone Age—the AI Stone Age, that is—as we cover the history of computational devices and unravel the mystery of machine learning and conversational AI. After our crash course on what artificial intelligence is (and what it isn't), we'll dive on through the digital looking glass as we enter into the era of ChatGPT proper. We'll outline the strengths and limitations of AI's poster child before beginning to define how you can begin using it to enhance both your personal and professional life.

As we'll come to see, ChatGPT is the best personal assistant (PA) you could ever ask for. With its ability to process natural language combined with its deep learning capacity, this revolutionary chatbot can assist you with project management, content creation, and more—even serving as your therapist-on-demand to assist with keeping on top of your mental health. Besides these more personal uses, you can also use it to take your professional life up a few levels, serving as your pocket-sized business partner. After we've dipped our toes into the waters of what ChatGPT can do with these more well-known uses of assistive AI, we'll dive in deeper as we see how you can incorporate the technology into your daily life before we push generative AI to its (mildly sarcastic) limits. Finally, we'll end our journey off with some wooing words from your witty new AI pal and see how, contrary to popular belief, it can actually enhance technological accessibility for all, rather than increasing the digital divide.

As with every new technological invention we humans create, it's your choice whether to use it to improve your life, or lose out and be left behind. ChatGPT and conversational AI are here to stay. So why not learn how to use them to their full potential, while simultaneously safeguarding yourself from the potential risks they can have? That's what this book—your perfect companion in navigating the world of chatbots and AI—is here for. Read on, learn to ride the techno-wave, and ensure that you are future-proof and ship-shape for sailing the high seas of productivity, as well as personal and professional improvement. The world is your oyster, especially when you've got your ultimate assistant, ChatGPT, on your side. It's time to begin our adventure with Chapter 1: When Bots Start Talking Back.

Chapter 1
When Bots Start Talking Back

Ever wonder how we went from simple number-crunching machines to advanced conversational AIs? What about how we invented those number-crunching machines in the first place? Well, my fine chat maestro in the making, welcome to your crash course into the history of computers, the revolution of machine learning, and the evolution of chatbots.

We'll begin our foray into the annals of history by returning to the Stone Age. Not the one we humans went through all those thousands of years ago, but the one that our creation—artificial intelligence—went through a lot more recently. Once we've talked about computers the size of rooms, and Alan Turing's groundbreaking concept of "machines that can think," we'll then take a trip through early processing languages, its evolution into machine learning algorithms, and finally, end off in the modern day with the rise of AI chatbots (no need to think of Terminator taking over, I assure you!). After that, we'll decode some of the jargon you'll need to know going forward and outline the characteristics of our friendly neighborhood AI.

Finally, we'll end off this first chapter into the world of mastering AI conversations by talking about the techno-elephant in the room: OpenAI and its language model, GPT-4. By the end of this chapter, you'll not only be able to impress your friends at dinner parties with your in-depth understanding of the history of artificial intelligence and machine learning, but you will be a lot more comfortable with ChatGPT and using it to improve every part of your life. Don't be a doomsday prepper; embrace the future of humankind by learning how to use this powerful evolutionary tool we call AI. As we shall see, ChatGPT and its siblings are as revolutionary a tool for man as was the invention of our very first tools way back in the original Stone Age.

Back to the AI Stone Age

We humans have always felt the need to measure and quantify things. In the earliest of times, BC (before computers), we used whatever was around to help us count and keep track of what we had. Sticks, stones, bones, shells, and various other things found around, or on the ground, were used to compute what we couldn't store in our heads. According to the good ol' dictionary, the word compute means, to "reckon or calculate (a figure or amount)." The more informal (but still dictionary approved) definition of the word is, "seem reasonable; make sense." In other words, to compute means to figure something out, or to make sense of the world around us.

Early Computing Devices

As humans advanced and our world became ever more complicated, we needed to develop more complex ways of working things out. While it was a long way before the first computer was invented (we're still talking BC here, after all!), we did devise different devices to help us keep up with our own progress. As technology improved and the human intellect grew, these computing devices became able to not only calculate more, but also capable of doing a vast variety of computational tasks. To give you an overview of how we went from counting sticks and stones to developing the first machine called a computer, let's go through some of these early computing devices and their uses:

1. The abacus

One ancient society that was really ahead of the game in terms of technological advancements was the Chinese. Not only did the ancient Chinese invent paper, gunpowder, clocks, and even compasses, but 4,000 years ago, they also invented a computational device that is the forefather of all calculators: the abacus. Consisting of a wooden frame with metal poles running horizontally along it, the abacus worked by moving beads spread out along the metal poles, following certain guidelines or rules (or algorithms, if you like). This would then be used to compute arithmetic (addition and subtraction), and allowed us to keep track of larger amounts without needing them in front of us to count.

2. Napier's bones

Jumping ahead to the early 1600s in Scotland, we see our next major advancement in computing devices. Invented by John Napier, Napier's bones used nine ivory strips—the bones—that were etched with numbers. While the abacus allowed us to add and subtract better than ever before, Napier's bones added to this the ability to multiply and divide. It also allowed for the use of the decimal point system, a first for our early computational devices.

3. Pascaline

Next up in the history of computing devices comes the Pascaline. Invented by renowned French philosopher and mathematician Blaise Pascal between 1642-1644, the Pascaline consisted of a wooden box with a bunch of gears inside. Pascals's father was a tax supervisor for Rouen, a city in northern France, and had a tough time staying on top of all the arithmetical calculations he had to make in order to ensure that "death and taxes" remained the only two certainties of life. To help his daddy-o out with this, Pascal created the first mechanical and automated calculator.

4. Difference engine and analytical engine

With the first few iterations of human computational devices covered, we now get to the ones created by the "father of the computer," English polymath Charles Babbage. Invented in the early 1820s, Babbage's difference engine could do more than just the single simple calculations of its predecessors. It could compute a series of calculations with a number of variables, allowing us to solve much more complicated mathematical equations. More than that though, the difference engine was also able to store data to process at a later stage (albeit temporarily), as well as to print out its solutions. This marked a clear separation of the difference engine from other calculators of the day, however Babbage's machine (which was the size of a room) was still only able to do one task at a time.

Then, in 1830, Babbage developed his next mechanical computer, the analytical engine. While the difference engine was considered a calculating machine, the analytical engine is generally thought of as being the world's first computer. The big difference between the difference and analytical engines is that, while the former was only able to do one task at a time and was still limited in terms of its calculation abilities, the latter was a general-purpose computing machine able to complete any and all calculations put to it. Unlike its predecessor, the analytical engine was also able to store data indefinitely.

The analytical engine was made of four different parts, which are still the main elements of the modern computers that we use today. The first, the mill, was its calculating unit and is the grandfather of the central processing unit (CPU) that we find in our computers. The next component Babbage called the store, and was where data was kept before being processed. This corresponds to memory and storage in modern computers and similar devices. Third up, we have the reader (the input device), with the final component being the printer (the output device).

5. The tabulating machine

Our next iteration leading up to the modern-day computer and the birth of artificial intelligence was the tabulating machine. Invented around 60 years after the analytical engine by German-American statistician Herman Hollerith, the tabulating machine was a counting machine originally used to organize U.S. census data in 1890. By counting cards where holes were punched at specific locations, Hollerith's invention could work out statistics and then sort and record data. This made it perfect for accounting or keeping track of inventory, and led to a new category of computing machines known as unit recording equipment, as well as a new industry: data processing. Hollerith created a company for his invention, which would eventually evolve into International Business Machines, more commonly known today as IBM. IBM would create the first completely electronic computing machine—the Vacuum Tube Multiplier—in 1943, and a year later, would produce the Mark I, the first device that we would recognize as being a modern computer.

6. Mark I

Built in the U.S. toward the end of the Second World War, the Automatic Sequence Controlled Calculator, more commonly called the Harvard Mark I, was developed by Professor Howard Aiken from Harvard University in collaboration with IBM. Aiken was fascinated with Babbage's analytical engine, and like the analytical engine, the Mark I was a behemoth of a machine. Weighing in at a whopping 5 tons, 50 feet (15 meters) long,

Aiken's invention was made up of over 750,000 different parts and hundreds of miles of wire. As its inputs and output, the Mark I had three paper-tape readers, two card readers, one punch card, and two typewriters, and it took between three to six seconds to perform simple calculations. One of the first uses of the Mark I was as part of the Manhattan Project where it was used to help calculate whether implosion (violently collapsing) was a good idea to detonate the atomic bomb. Aiken went on to make three more versions of his machine (Mark I–IV), mainly used for militaristic purposes.

The History of Early AI and Chatbots

Now that we know the origins of the tools and devices that led to the creation of the modern-day computer, it's time to look at the history of AI and chatbots. We'll continue our story from the AI Stone Age to the modern day with the Turing revolution and the first time machines were thought of as being able to think. After that, we'll turn to the creation of the earliest language processing systems and the revolutionary concept of machine learning. Catching up with the modern era, we'll end this history lesson with a look into the various ways we use AI today, showing just how much our creation has evolved from the early computational devices we covered above. Get your thinking brain ready, because it's about to get artificially intelligent up in here!

Stranger Than Science Fiction: The Three Laws of Robotics

As we've just seen, it was in the late 19th and early 20th century that the first generation of the "thinking machines" we today call computers came about. While these ancestors of modern-day AI weren't able to do much more than basic computational tasks, mainly to do with calculations, they were absolutely groundbreaking at the time. Within certain circles, that is. It wouldn't be until Steve Jobs and Apple in the 1980s that computers and AI became accessible to the average Joe. Before that, AI was almost completely in the realm of mathematicians, scientists, philosophers, the military, and science fiction writers. While the last category of those involved in AI might not seem so obvious, think about this: We told stories about what it might be like to walk on the moon hundreds of years before we first stepped foot on its hallowed surface. The big question on all of these early AI enthusiasts' minds, especially in the first half of the 20th century, was: "Can machines think?"

In the early 1900s, a bunch of stories began to be released dealing with this very question. The Tin Man from L. Frank Baum's *Wizard of Oz* and the humanoid robot from Thea von Harbou's *Metropolis* are just two early examples of the way storytellers tried to get their heads around the future of these machines that were able to think for themselves. Another early adopter of the idea that machines would one day become intelligent was American writer and professor of biochemistry, Isaac Asimov. Asimov began writing about the rise of AI in the early 1940s, originally publishing his short story *Liar!* in the May 1941 edition of *Astounding Science Fiction*, which he would later republish into a collection called *I, Robot* in 1950. This book was used as inspiration for the 2004 movie released under the same name and introduces the Three Laws of Robotics, a set of rules created by Asimov that outlined how robots should operate within human society. It is also considered the first time that the word "robotics" was used.

This prolific science fiction writer's three laws are still considered a template, or at the very least, inspiration guiding the development of robots, machine learning, and AI to this day. In 2007, the government of South Korea even created their Robot Ethics Charter based on Asimov's laws. While they may need updating for the 21st century (there was no way that Asimov could possibly have predicted just how far and fast AI would advance), they still form an essential part of the groundwork for anyone looking to learn about machine learning and artificial intelligence. Asmiov's Three Laws are:

1. A robot may not injure a human being or, through inaction, allow a human being to come to harm.
2. A robot must obey the orders given to it by human beings, except where such orders conflict with the First Law.
3. A robot must protect its own existence as long as such protection does not conflict with the First or Second Laws.

Science fiction was the first way that the general public became familiarized with the idea that artificially intelligent robots could be on the cards in the near future. It might have taken longer than these early science fiction writers thought for us to get to the stage of walking, talking robots, but we are here today. Besides, what ChatGPT and the other forms of AI that are the norm in the world of today can do, would blow the minds of these early pioneers.

Alan Turing and the Turing Test

One of these early AI pioneers was the British polymath, Alan Turing. Turing was fascinated with what computers could do, as well as what they would be able to do in the future. As such, he began to investigate the mathematical possibilities of artificial intelligence and how far (and how fast) it would evolve. Turing began his exploration of what AI could one day evolve into by considering what humans are currently capable of doing. From his viewpoint, if humans can use the information available to us, as well as logic and reasoning, to solve complicated problems and reach informed decisions, then why shouldn't machines be able to learn to do the same thing? And so, he set out to answer this question as best he could. In 1950, Turing released a groundbreaking research paper called *Computing Machinery and Intelligence*, wherein he outlined his hypothesis for how artificial intelligence could be built, as well as how we could test just how intelligent these machines were. Enter the Turing Test.

While you'd think that the test of how intelligent robots are would be complicated, it's actually pretty simple. The key tenet behind it is that if a machine is capable of having a conversation with a human, without said human being able to detect that it's a robot, then it has shown enough intelligence to pass the Turing Test. Turing began to work on his trailblazing brand of computer science while working on ways to break German coded messages during World War II. After the war, Turing took his developing theory and put it to answering the question: "Can machines think?"

A Conversation Between Two Early Chatbots

It took much quicker than you would think for someone to create an AI that stood a chance of passing the Turing Test. The first contender was ELIZA, an early chatbot created in 1966 by computer scientist Joseph Weizenbaum. ELIZA's main function was to search for specific keywords used in conversations between different human typists. Weizenbaum's chatbot would then add those keywords to its dataset and use them to form full sentences, respond to questions asked of it, or even ask questions of its own. ELIZA's aim was to act as a psychotherapist, which in Weizenbaum's words, allowed it to take the position of "knowing almost nothing of the real world." If the human ELIZA was chatting to used one of the keywords in its set, then the chatbot would use that word in its response. If no keywords were found, then it would just give a generic response that it thought fit the bill.

In 1972, a psychiatrist from Stanford University named Kenneth Colby created the next contender for passing the Turing Test: PARRY. Colby described his chatbot as "ELIZA with attitude," and seemed to have created it in direct competition to Weizenbaum's AI. While ELIZA was designed to replicate a human psychologist, PARRY was modeled to mimic the behavior of a paranoid schizophrenic. After a group of 33 human psychologists "trained" PARRY, they used a variation of the Turing Test to check how Colby's chatbot would measure up. And lo and behold, PARRY managed to score a passing grade, successfully fooling 52% of people into thinking that it was an actual human.

Then, a year later at an international computer conference, the two bots met for a chat. Using ARPANET—the Advanced Research Projects Agency Network, one the world's first computer networks—as their platform, the psychologist met with the paranoid schizophrenic. What followed was one of the weirdest conversations in AI history. While we don't have the space to cover the convo in full, it's interesting to look at how it began and how it ended. It went as follows (Garber, 2014):

How it began:

> ELIZA: Good evening. Tell me your problems. Please terminate input with a period or a question mark.
> PARRY: People get on my nerves sometimes.
> ELIZA: I am not sure I understand you fully.
> PARRY: You should pay more attention.
> ELIZA: Suppose you should pay more attention.
> PARRY: You're entitled to your own opinion.
> ELIZA: What makes you think I am entitled to my own opinion?
> PARRY: It bothers me just to be around people in general.
> ELIZA: Please go on.

How it ended:

> PARRY: You are a real nag.
> ELISA: Does it please you to believe I am a real nag?

PARRY: I have had enough of this.

ELISA: What does that suggest to you?

PARRY: Goodbye.

ELISA: It's been my pleasure, that's $399.29 please.

The Revolutionary Concept of Machine Learning

The above conversation between these two early language processing systems might seem like a funny chat between a disinterested psychologist and a grumpy schizo, but it was pretty revolutionary in terms of what it meant for the world of computing and AI. And, while many debate whether ELIZA and PARRY really passed the Turing Test due to Turing's tenet that they should be able to repeatedly fool people into thinking they're actually human rather than just a once off, they marked a definite advancement in artificial intelligence and machine learning. But what exactly does the term "machine learning" mean? And why was it so revolutionary for the advancement of robotkind (oh, and humankind too)?

Let's start with the definition. A branch of artificial intelligence, machine learning allows computers to learn through experience and improve their systems without programmers updating their code. This leads AI to being more accurate in its ability to predict outcomes related to its central function. There are many functional applications for machine learning in almost every industry out there, from self-driving cars to social media marketing. It's also the reason why we have ELIZA, PARRY, and of course, ChatGPT in the first place!

According to a 2020 survey conducted by Deloitte, one of the "big four" accounting firms, more than 67% of companies operating today use some form of machine learning in their daily operations, with that percentage growing year-in, year-out (Brown, 2021). As we saw from the Turing Test and the conversation between our first two chatbots, the main aim of AI (and of computational devices in general) is to take up the grunt work historically done by us humans. We used to have to count things ourselves, until we invented machines to count for us. We used to have to solve problems and predict trends ourselves, until we invented algorithms to do that for us. We used to have to think and speak for ourselves, until… you get the picture.

While many members of the general public are worried about just how far we're going to let AI take over the tasks of the average Joe, businesses are buying into the AI automation revolution full throttle. Business-wise, it just makes sense. And as we'll see in the chapters to come, it's not nearly as scary or doomsday-esque as the fear-mongers among us would have you believe. All it takes is learning how to use it correctly.

A Crash Course Into Machine Learning

The best way to think about machine learning is: As the means by which artificial intelligence learns to do more complicated tasks, becomes more accurate at performing its programmed functions, and solves problems that will help make human life simpler. All without its creator (aka the programmer) having to oversee every aspect of its improvement like a helicopter parent. Speaking of parents, the person who first coined the term "machine learning" was professor Emeritus Arthur

Samuel, the artificial intelligence and computer gaming pioneer who proved that machines can learn from the past. The way that Samuel demonstrated that machines can learn was through the game of checkers.

In 1956, he created a computer program that could play checkers to run on the IBM 701. He was under the impression that fellow computer scientist and "father of the information theory" Claude Shannon, had built a similar style program, but for chess. When Samuel met Shannon a few years later, however, he discovered that Shannon had only described the possibility of making such a program for chess in an article published in *Scientific American.* And so it was, that Arthur Samuel became the accidentally on-purpose inventor of the field of machine learning, and checkers the game, not chess (although the chess version of Samuel's Checkers program was soon in the making).

Then, in 1962, the self-proclaimed checkers champion Robert Nealey sat down at an IBM 7094 computer and challenged Arthur Samuel's Checkers program to a match. The computer won. While Samuel's machine learning AI didn't win every game that it played, especially not at the beginning, it did *learn* from every game.

The Big Shift in Machine Learning

With the Turing Test "successes" of the early chatbots ELIZA and PARRY, and the victory of Arthur Samuel's Checkers program over a man who called himself champion, artificial intelligence and its exponential applications began to buzz around the world. There were many other AI success stories in the 1970s and 1980s, but the next real big push in the world of artificial intelligence came in the 1990s. And it all had to do with the advancement of machine learning.

In 1989, machine learning left university life and got itself a job as it became one of the core algorithms in the first personal computer (PC). The commercialization of machine learning was done by Axcelis Inc. in its Evolver software package, which put some money numbers to the use of its genetic algorithms on the newly released personal computers (the first of which was released in 1971).

With the massive success of the PC, excitement around machine learning and its capabilities grew from the world of academia to the world of business. It didn't leave the world of academics, obviously, as it also continued to flourish at universities; but machine learning now had external funding, and the pockets of those external funders were deep and plentiful. In 1997, the world champion of chess lost not to a specific computer scientist's program, but to IBM (International Business Machine)'s Deep Blue.

Another big shift for machine learning came in the '90s as machine learning shifted from knowledge to data driven. This was mainly due to the mass volumes of information that had been collected by this stage. The difference between a knowledge-based system and a data-based system is quite large. For one thing, where knowledge bases are used to make external resources, share information, and support the decision-making process, databases are used to store and organize data internally so that it can be retrieved with ease, if and when the algorithm (not the human) requires it to make a more informed decision. In other words, this big shift in machine learning came about as we trusted AI to take care of more and more of the problem-solving process.

Machine Learning in the Early 21st Century

Speeding up our whirlwind history through the evolution of machine learning a decade or so, our next big improvement comes in 2012 with the creation of Google Brain. A deep neural network, Google Brain greatly advanced AI's ability to recognize patterns, allowing it to interpret more and more complex images and videos. This algorithm would be put to work in detecting objects and recognizing patterns in YouTube videos, ensuring as little illegal or indecent material as possible found its way onto the platform. The pattern recognition advancements of AI continued as Facebook put its own machine learning algorithm, Deep Face, to work on recognising people's faces in pictures, allowing for easy tagging of friends in photos. Released in 2014, Deep Face was another groundbreaking development in machine learning. By this stage, AI had learned to recognize people just as accurately as humans do.

Also released in 2014 was a program called *AlphaGo* by Deep Mind. Created to play *Go*, largely considered the most complicated game we humans have managed to design, *AlphaGo* managed the same result as its predecessors did with chess and checkers: It defeated a human who considered themselves a champion. Then, in 2015, a company called OpenAI entered the scene whose sole purpose was to create "safe and friendly AI that could benefit humanity." From this day on, artificial intelligence and machine learning became mainstream.

Decoding the Jargon: AI Characteristics

With AI going mainstream, we now reach the modern day of intelligent machines and software programs that have no issue whatsoever in passing the Turing Test. Through artificial intelligence and chatbots, we're creating applications that can accurately replicate the way the human brain works. This means that AI now has the same problem-solving, rationalizing, reasoning, planning, perceiving, and of course, decision-making capabilities of the average person. In fact, I'd wager a lot better. The ability of AI to outperform humans is no longer news; it's history. And, with the growing amount of people researching ways to make AI smarter and more lifelike, and more money coming in from the private sector, the field of machine learning has skyrocketed. The robot business is booming, so make sure you get in on the gold rush and aren't left behind in the dust.

What AI Is

With the history of AI and machine learning covered from the Stone Age to the modern day, it's now time to cover its main characteristics. We now know how AI was invented, but what exactly is it made up of? Let's get under the hood and learn about the main components of artificial intelligence.

Feature Engineering

The first characteristic of artificial intelligence is feature engineering. Also called feature extraction, this is the process by which AI sifts through large amounts of data and extracts features (common trends in the dataset). Feature extraction allows data to be classified and categorized, bringing order to the dataset and allowing easy analysis. It also allows you (or the program itself) to easily isolate a particular trend or feature. This was pivotal to the mass advancement of machine learning.

Artificial Neural Networks

Artificial neural networks (ANNs) might sound like a mouthful of a phrase, but they're actually quite simple. Our brains, for example, are neural networks. So, another way to think of artificial neural networks is as a robot brain. The ability to create artificial neural networks arose directly out of advancements in machine learning. In fact, it's considered a branch of machine learning and is at the core of the deep learning algorithms that we'll go over next. Another name for ANNs is SNNs (simulated neural networks), because the inspiration for structuring and designing these artificial networks came, surprise surprise, from copying the way that neurons send signals to one another in the biological neural network: the human brain.

These neural networks are dependent on the quantity and quality of the training data you give it. This is because they are based on machine learning algorithms and require simulations (from the dataset and from experiential training) to improve their accuracy over time. Once these algorithms have all the data they need and have fine-tuned their accuracy, they develop just like our own neural pathways grow the more we do something.

Deep Learning

As artificial neural networks developed, they became more and more complicated. Very soon, they surpassed the capabilities of what the best human is capable of, and continued on. Layer after layer, ANNs continued to grow until they formed what we call a deep learning network. Deep learning is the latest buzzword in AI circles, and is the algorithm behind the driverless cars being developed at the moment, as well as ChatGPT. While machine learning requires a human to input the features and upload the data for the algorithm to classify, deep learning does not.

Natural Language Processing

In order for machines to "chat" to us, they need to use words that we are familiar with. In other words, AI has to be able to process natural, everyday language not only on the input (computing information), but also on the output (telling us about that information). When AI took in information in the past, it was usually in the form of numbers. As we saw earlier on in this chapter, all of the early computational devices were made to help us keep track of numbers, solve mathematical equations, and isolate trends in datasets. Nowadays though, computers do a whole lot more than just crunch numbers. Through machine learning, AI is now fluent in all human languages, both spoken and written. It can respond to questions, generate new text based on requests, and even translate between languages faster than the world's best polyglot. Although AI at the moment might not have the same fluency as a native speaker, it's only a matter of time, thanks to the subfield of machine learning called natural language processing.

Intelligent Robotics

When you were a kid, did you ever watch a program called *Robot Wars*? If not, you should check it out, it's just a short YouTube search away. The British game show ran from 1998-2018 and had a very simple premise: People built robots and battled them against one another in a "winner takes all" style of oilshed and mayhem. Robots of the future will look back at these early ancestors of theirs as we do the gladiators that fought in the arenas of Rome.

Jokes aside, *Robot Wars* is the perfect example of what intelligent robotics is all about. A combination of engineering and computer science, robotics deals with creating programmable machines (robots) that can help people or can copy human actions. At first, robotics just dealt with making machines that could do very basic, monotonous tasks such as those "conveyor belt" jobs, like assembly-line work, packaging, and so on. Working their way up from the factory line, robots are now programmed to take care of domestic tasks (think of Smart Homes and Siri, your household assistant), jobs in the world of commerce (your banking apps), and even serving their country in the military (classified).

Perception

Not only do our machines of the future need to think, walk, and talk, but they also need to be able to perceive the world around them. This is trickier than you may think for a robot to do, but the tech is getting there. Using sensors (cameras, wireless signals, microphones, etc.) as opposed to senses (hearing, feeling, seeing, tasting, and smelling), machines are learning to better perceive the world around them. Great advancements in machine perception have been made, especially in software programmed for recognizing speech, faces, and objects. Which leads us to our final characteristic of modern-day AI…

Facial Recognition

If you've ever wondered how AI can recognize your beautiful visage from all the other ugly mugs out there, it's all thanks to biometric mapping. Biometrics means "biological measurements," and is the way AI identifies people through their physical characteristics. One of the most well-known uses of facial recognition software is to help us tag our friends on Facebook using the knowledge it's given (i.e., the photos) and comparing them to its database of faces. Besides the socials, facial recognition software is also used by businesses to help authenticate their employee's identity or other job roles that require ID verification of people.

Common Misconceptions About AI and Machine Learning

Now that we've gone over the main things that make up modern-day AI, it's time to go over all the things that AI definitely isn't. Everyone from your great-grandma to Elon Musk is busy sounding the warning call of the "robots taking over," but how true is this, and how much of it is just scaremongering? With Sam Altman, CEO of OpenAI, openly predicting that computer programs will very soon be able to do everything that a human is capable of, can we call the techno doomsday preppers correct that this spells the end for humanity? Or, is there still the chance that we can keep control over our creation and stop the lynching of Frankenstein's monster? As we shall see, whether or not AI destroys us depends more on how correctly informed the angry mob is, rather than on how "good" our creation is. In other words, if we don't want AI to destroy us, then we should stop trying to destroy it. The first step? Do your research and learn to separate the facts from the fiction. As such, let's go over some of the common misconceptions surrounding artificial intelligence and machine learning.

The Machines Are Taking Over

For many who grew up watching movies like *The Terminator, The Matrix,* and *Ex Machina,* the dawn of artificial intelligence marks the doom of the human race. But it doesn't have to be that way. We just have to change the way we think of AI, from being a part of the problem to being part of the solution. The way Massachusetts Institute of Technology (MIT) tech researcher Kate Darling thinks about AI in her book, *The New Breed: How to Think About Robots,* is quite interesting, for example. Rather than viewing machines as Homo-Sapien 2.0, Darling says we should view them as a new breed of animal. And, just like humans have worked alongside horses, dogs, and other domesticated animals for centuries without worrying that they'll take over, we shouldn't feel the need to compete against AI. Before you say, "but a horse didn't take any human jobs," yes, yes it did. Who do you think pulled the carts and plows *before* we started using horses to do that for us?

AI Will Steal Jobs

This brings us onto the second common misconception that people have about AI, and that is, "if it doesn't kill us, it's going to take my job!" This is a worry that more and more industries are experiencing, as the abilities of AI and machine learning seem to be ever growing and expanding. While it's true that AI will, and is, changing the very way that we work, it's not true that it's going to leave all people behind in the dust bowl as it does so. The AI revolution, just like every other form of industrial revolution that came before it, will mean that some jobs are lost or transformed in the process. But it's important to remember that this is nothing new, and just like the times before, it will most likely not lead to a reduction of the overall number of jobs available, but rather an increase.

One of the previous large shifts in the job world came from robotization, where machines took over the repetitive industrial jobs previously done by humans. We can think of the recent advancements in artificial intelligence as eliminating repetitive "intellectual" jobs and tasks, such as those to do with categorizing data or sifting through large datasets for specific information or trends. This frees up our time and helps us to work in a faster, more efficient, more intelligent way.

AI Has Surpassed Human Intelligence

Linked to fears that AI's going to take our jobs are fears that AI is also smarter than us. Many of us already feel belittled, bordering on bewildered, when it comes to the complexity of the tech being developed today. Add in the fact that AI just seems to be getting smarter, and you have a double-whammy of human insecurity. But fear not! Because AI is not smarter than a fifth-grader. Not yet, at least.

Now, before you jump down my throat by saying that an AI can definitely know more than the average 10 year-old, let me just clarify something. Sure, an AI can gather loads of information and respond to very specific questions or solve highly focused problems, but in terms of what we call generalized intelligence, it's severely lacking. Artificial intelligence is still not able to tackle an indefinite number of different tasks at once, for example. While it may not always remain this way, human intelligence or natural intelligence-levels for robots, still belongs to the realm of science fiction.

OpenAI and Its Language Model, GPT-4

With the characteristics of artificial intelligence and machine learning outlined and the common misconceptions surrounding it covered, it's now time to hone our focus in on the main topic for this book: That buzzword of 2023, ChatGPT. In this final section to the first chapter, we'll be learning the story behind this powerful language model and the company that created it.

OpenAI, the Company Behind ChatGPT

We've mentioned the name OpenAI once or twice in this chapter so far. With the mission statement of creating "safe and friendly AI that could benefit humanity," OpenAI has come a long way since it was founded eight years ago in San Francisco.

To begin our story of this non-profit company sharing open-source products, let's take a trip back to 2015 to discover why exactly it was founded in the first place, and by who.

In December 2015, a few of the biggest names in the tech world, as well as a couple unknowns, got together to create a company aimed at creating artificial general intelligence that was not only useful, but also as smart as a human (in certain specific tasks set to it). In fact, according to OpenAI's charter, reaching the same level of intelligence was only the stepping stone to their true goal of designing "highly autonomous systems that outperform humans at most economically valuable work" (OpenAI, 2018).

The people behind the company were Sam Altman (co-founder of Loopt, short-time CEO of Reddit, and CEO of OpenAI), Greg Brockman (MIT graduate, former CTO of the financial services company Stripe, and current president of OpenAI), Wojciech Zaremba (computer scientist and leader of OpenAI's codex research and language teams), John Schulman (research scientist and leader of the reinforcement learning team), and Elon Musk (former chairman and CEO of the company, now part-time CTO and board member). The ambitious task that brought them all together? Creating safe AI tools made available to the general public that would empower people to work more effectively and efficiently, rather than eradicate their jobs.

The main two founders to spearhead the project for safe AI development, open to the general public, were Sam Altman and Elon Musk. While Musk was highly involved at the beginning of the initiative (making a $10 million cash contribution to the company in 2016), he left the board in 2018. While the exact reason for his departure is not entirely known, Musk has made clear that he doesn't believe that the rest of the OpenAI team were as dedicated to ensuring that the machines they designed were "safe." Another reason, the one officially stated by Musk, was the overlap of roles he played in OpenAI and one of its main competitors in the field of machine learning: Tesla. Even though they had lost Musk, and with him, the majority of their funding, OpenAI didn't just survive, but began to thrive.

Enter GPT

ChatGPT's mind vast,

Answers flow with ease

AI's tongue at last.

— ChatGPT

In 2018, the same year that Musk left the company, OpenAI published a research paper titled *Improving Language Understanding by Generative Pre-Training*. While this may sound like a mouthful of a paper title, the important part of it lies in the final two words: generative pre-training. This was the first time the concept of a generative pre-trained transformer was put forward, an idea that would lead to the AI revolution we're experiencing at the moment. If you haven't figured it out yet, the acronym of generative pre-trained transformer is GPT.

So, what exactly are GPTs? To put it simply, they are neural networks trained using a massive dataset of text generated by humans. Remember that another example of a neural network is the human brain. This is what machine learning programs like those of ChatGPT are modeled on. GPT-1, OpenAI's first attempt at creating their chatbot, was "trained" using BookCorpus, a dataset of over 11,000 unpublished books. GPT-2 grew on this dataset, and using its more powerful programming, added eight million web pages to its growing repository of information. These web pages contained around 1.5 billion parameters, which are the historical data that GPTs use to determine the best response to give, or the next best word to put (aka, predictive text). GPT-3, released in 2022, contained 175 billion parameters, more than 10 times more than its predecessor and totaling more than 570 gigabytes of information. In order to handle the processing power necessary to "house" GPT-3, Microsoft designed OpenAI a supercomputer, which was the fifth most powerful supercomputer when it was released.

Then, in November 2022, OpenAI released ChatGPT, a language model chatbot that used GPT's neural network as its base. We'll go over all the tips and tricks, perks and pitfalls to this powerful chatbot in the chapters to come, but for now, we're just going to put out a teaser of what makes ChatGPT an AI and machine learning revolution in its own right. Unlike anything that came before it, ChatGPT has the ability to understand context. This means that it can learn and adapt within a single conversation, generating results to the questions you ask it, tailored according to the history of your chat. This also means that, within a single conversation thread, you can "train" GPT to produce more and more accurate answers, or, to write more and more in your preferred style.

Welcome to the other side of the AI looking glass, and step on through to chapter two.

Chapter 2
Through the Looking Glass

By this stage, I'm sure you've realized that ChatGPT isn't just some new piece of code—it's your new best friend. This natural language processing chatbot contains 300 billion words of information from the internet, books, news, blogs, and more. This is around 16 times more information than the average human can consume within their lifetime. And, with its deep machine learning models, it's only getting better at using its 570 gigs of info to make your life easier. The collaboration of ChatGPT's language learning models, along with its massive database, means that it can both understand the prompts, questions, and commands you give it, as well as respond with accurate answers in the blink of an eye. This makes it the perfect digital assistant for finding detailed information on any topic under the sun. And, as we shall see, it can do much more than just that.

In this chapter, we're going to get properly under the hood of this fantastic digital assistant for the 21st century. Beginning with an overview of the architecture and functions of AI's poster child, we'll then highlight the unique strengths of ChatGPT compared to other machine learning algorithms, looking into real-life examples of how ChatGPT has successfully helped both individuals and businesses to become bigger and better than ever before. Once that's done, it's time to get to the heart of the machine as we learn about prompt engineering. But, as great as ChatGPT may be, nothing in this world is perfect, and AI is no exception. That's why we'll end this chapter off with a lil' look into the limitations of this revolutionary technology. Step on through to the other side of the AI looking glass as we learn what makes it tick.

Architecture and Functioning of ChatGPT

In the previous chapter, we went over the history of the company that created the generative pre-trained transformers we call GPTs, OpenAI, as well as the first few iterations of their deep-learning programs, GPT 1, 2, and 3. Let's pick up where we left off with the release of ChatGPT and the fourth evolution of the GPT software.

What Can GPT-4 Do?

We've covered a lot of the spec-based info surrounding these crazy cool things called GPTs, but what exactly can these deep learning models do? Well, almost any information-based task you set it, really. And, the more you "chat" to the GPT about a particular topic, the more fine-tuned your answers and results will get. While there are almost as many applications for

ChatGPT as there are questions in the human mind, let's quickly list out the most common uses of this powerful new computer program:

- Answer questions.
- Summarize text.
- Translate text.
- Create code.
- Generate ready-made blogs, conversations, or any content type that a human can ask it to do.

In March 2023, OpenAI released their latest version of their text-generating AI, GPT-4. There were a number of improvements made between GPT-3 and the fourth version, including the GPT-3.5 series during which the conversation generating chatbot called ChatGPT was released. While GPT–4 was an upgrade of the 3.5 model, the upgrades made were crucial to its continued success with the general public. The ChatGPT running on GPT-3.5 wasn't always factually correct, often wrote offensive material, and was becoming a problem not only for OpenAI, but also for the people using it.

As such, GPT-4 was labeled a model "alignment" upgrade. In other words, aligning ChatGPT more with good than with evil, and making sure that what it states as fact lines up with the truth. Other than better alignment with the morals of civilized society, the fourth iteration also saw an improved ability to follow the intentions and adapt to the behavior of its users. This is called the "steerability" of machine learning software. The final step to bringing ChatGPT fully back in line with what is expected of a respectable algorithm was putting in place enforced restrictions. In other words, if someone were to, say, ask ChatGPT to do something illegal or produce something unsavory, it's now much better at saying no.

Besides bringing the program back in line, another major update GPT received was that GPT-4 can recognize not only text, but images too. And, as they say, a picture speaks a thousand words. So far, GPT-4 has been able to correctly identify charts and graphs, memes, and even screenshots taken of complex academic papers.

GPT-4 is also a much better problem solver than its predecessors. Both GPT-3.5 and GPT-4 had to go through rigorous schooling, including sitting their high-school SATs and advanced placement tests, then moving on to their college graduate record examination (GREs), before finally sitting the lawyer's bar exam. They then branched out into sommelier exams to become wine stewards with law degrees. GPT-4 outperformed its predecessor in all aspects, achieving human-level scores in almost everything. Though there was one subject that GPT-4 just couldn't get: English language and literature.

AI's Poster Child: Strengths of ChatGPT

As we've seen so far, ChatGPT is one groundbreaking piece of work. In the short time since its release, it has already pushed the boundaries of what AI is capable of, setting into motion the next wave in AI innovation and technological development: What we could call AI's conversational revolution. Bill Gates, the founder of Microsoft and the world's sixth richest man, once commented that ChaptGPT is one of two technological steps forward that he would consider to be revolutionary. He went on to say, "[ChatGPT] inspired me to think about all the things that AI can achieve in the next five to ten years" (Rampton, 2023).

"It will change the way people work, learn, travel, get health care, and communicate with each other. Entire industries will reorient around it. Businesses will distinguish themselves by how well they use it" (Rampton, 2023).

And Gates isn't alone in believing that ChatGPT is truly revolutionary. According to a study carried out by the Swiss bank UBS, ChatGPT is the "fastest-growing consumer application in history" (Gordon, 2023). Now that we've talked up the chatbot a bit, let's get to the specifics of what exactly makes it so great.

Think Tank Supreme

The first thing going for our poster child of the chatbot world, is the sheer amount of knowledge and information it has to draw on. Using its 570 gigs of data, it can provide detailed and knowledgeable information on almost any topic that you can think of.

Responsive AF

Not only does ChatGPT have a massive database to draw upon, but it can also provide answers quicker than it took you to type the question at hand. Not only that, but it can also accurately understand the underlying intent of a question, perform complex reasoning tasks, and produce creative, out-of-the-box pieces.

Fine-tunable and Personalizable

One of the most remarkable and revolutionary things about ChatGPT is that it can adapt within a single conversation thread. This fine-tunability allows more accurate, higher quality results without requiring endless prompting. It also means that ChatGPT can (in part) train itself on what you need, as it can tap into its dataset and use the examples that you provide it with in your prompt. The fine-tuning nature of our lil' chatbot also means that, the more you chat to it in a conversation thread, the more finessed its answers will become to your specific conversational style.

A Coder's Dream

In terms of technical strength, ChatGPT can make the lives of coders and web developers so much easier. It does this by saving them the most valuable currency out there: time. Through using the right prompts and putting in the correct parameters, ChatGPT can write code for you, speeding up the web development process. It can also assist with website testing by identifying any problems or issues with your site, as well as helping to debug and fix any coding errors that it may find (a personal specialty for ChatGPT). Finally, for us non-coders out there, it can make the world of website creation not only accessible, but doable. How? Well, you put in the prompt and enter the parameters using normal, everyday language, and it will produce the complicated coding side for you!

It's Free!

The final major strength of ChatGPT is that it's free and easily accessible to the general public. To gain access to this powerful PA of a chatbot, all you need to do is go to the OpenAI website or download its mobile app and sign up! No banking details or complicated contracts needed. Whatever ChatGPT produces for you does, however, automatically become training data to help it improve for the future, creating the perfect quid pro quo of man and machine.

Putting ChatGPT to Work

I'm sure you know enough about ChatGPT by now to be impressed, or at least to have your interest peaked. Let's carry on kindling those fires of interest and intrigue as we look at some of the top success stories from companies and people successfully putting ChatGPT to work making their lives better. We'll begin with the way large and well-known companies have integrated ChatGPT into their workflows and technical systems before covering how you (yes, you!) can put ChatGPT to work for you too.

Companies Successfully Using ChatGPT

If you're still thinking that ChatGPT is only useful to writers, researchers, and coders, then let's get the last of those cobwebs out of your eyes and help you to clearly see the true value of AI's chatbot poster child. It's important to remember that truly revolutionary tech, such as the PC, for example, found their way from the world of academics to the business world, and then through to the world of the everyday consumer (aka you and me). We've looked at how the academics created and used machine learning, deep learning, and chatbots, and now we're going to look into how businesses are doing so. Then, it's time to see how you and I can use it too.

▷ **Microsoft**

The first company we're going to look at is Microsoft. As we saw in the previous section, Microsoft's founder Bill Gates has been hot on ChatGPT and its potential applications since the very get-go. It's public knowledge that Microsoft is a major investor in OpenAI and that collaboration between the two companies has been growing. Bing, Microsoft's search engine run through Microsoft Edge, is now powered by the same large language models (LLMs) that run ChatGPT, namely GPT-3 and GPT-4. This opens up another way of surfing the web and searching for information. Rather than following the traditional route of entering a keyword and receiving a list of links, you can now search the web in a much more "chatty" style using the new conversational interface. Finally, Microsoft is also in the process of integrating LLMs into the Microsoft Suite. This means that soon programs like Word and Excel will have built-in versions of ChatGPT!

▷ **Duolingo**

The next company successfully putting ChatGPT to work is the tech-based language education company Duolingo. So far, the company has incorporated GPT-4 in two new features,

Duolingo Max and an AI "role-play" function. The first of these LLM-based features, Duolingo Max, allows students to receive feedback to incorrect test answers and in-depth explanations to any questions they have, all delivered in natural (and accurate) language that, by and large, is equatable to what they would have received from an actual tutor. The second feature might not have a catchy brand name, but is still pretty cool. It provides a platform for students to practice their language skills through taking part in role-play style activities with a wide variety of different AI "personas." Each persona has its own backstory and personality, which means you learn more about the AI's persona as you chat and practice your language skills.

▷ **Freshworks**

The customer service software company Freshworks has made great use of ChatGPT to improve its workflow. The LLM has allowed coders at Freshworks to reduce the time it takes to produce complex apps from 10 weeks down to one week or less. Talk about a boost to productivity! ChatGPT can code in a wide variety of popular coding languages, including the big three of C++, Python, and Javascript. Not only can it code in these languages, but it can also explain to others how the code it creates works, as well as how to debug it, if and when needed. In other words, ChatGPT is a master coder that can tutor others on how to code too.

▷ **Coca-Cola**

Yup, you read that right, even Coca-Cola is getting in on the ChatGPT game. The giant of the soft drink world has partnered with OpenAI, along with Bain & Company, to create a "first-of-its-kind AI platform" called "Create Real Magic" (Coca-Cola, 2023). This forms a part of Coca-Cola's new marketing push, created by Bain & Company, one of the "big three" management consultancy companies.

Combining ChatGPT with another of Open AI's deep learning machines, DALL-E, the platform allows users to "generate original artwork with iconic creative assets from the Coca-Cola archives" (Coca-Cola, 2023). And, if Coke likes the AI inspired art you create using their content and on their platform, they may just showcase it on their website or social channels. A fun business example of ChatGPT in action, and one that captures its more creative applications.

▷ **Snap Inc.**

The final company we're going to look at is Snap Inc., who have incorporated LLMs and conversational AI into their social media platform: Snapchat. Running under the name My AI, Snapchat's chatbot comes up as a normal contact on your friend's list and you can send it messages like you would your friends. Whether you want advice on what is the perfect gift to give your BFF, need help making plans for the long weekend, are struggling to decide what to have for dinner, or even just want some new kind of entertainment, My AI has you covered.

How You Can Successfully Start Using ChatGPT Too!

Now that we've seen just how successfully some of the biggest and brightest companies in the world have made their businesses better by adding ChatGPT to their daily operations, it's time to look at how individuals, like me and you, can do the same. We'll look at each of the ways you can get the most out of this powerful deep learning chatbot in a lot more detail in the chapters to follow, so think of this section as more of a taster of what's to come. As well as a cheat sheet as to how you can start taking action to include ChatGPT in your work and personal life straight away. Get ready, because it's time to learn how to empower your life with the power of ChatGPT!

▷ **Book and Blog Writing**

The first way that the average person can leverage ChatGPT is through its ability to generate text. Always had that novel idea at the back of your mind, but never had the time or the know-how to write it? Have an interesting life story perfect for a memoir, or are you a pro in your business niche with a lot of intel to share? Well then, my friend, ChatGPT could be just the digital PA you've been waiting for to launch your self-publishing career. Now, it's important to remember that the book our magical chatbot produces for you isn't going to be perfect. It won't reflect the levels of creativity or fluency that a native speaker of the language would be able to reach, but it will work for children's books or simple nonfiction books. Another thing that ChatGPT does well is short form writing, such as blogs or the like. It can also create one great outline.

▷ **Cover Letters and Resumes**

Besides helping boost your writing career, ChatGPT can also be extremely useful for updating the text in your curriculum vitae (CV) and keeping it updated. Getting all of your experience, qualifications, and previous job roles and responsibilities into an attractive and compelling snapshot of the professional person that is you can be pretty tough work. That is, until ChatGPT came along. All you have to do now, is enter in your experience and prompt the chatbot to turn it into something good. Then, sit back and watch the show. Not only can ChatGPT help to craft your CV, but it can also help write your cover letter for you, tailoring it for a new job application with the simple entering of a prompt.

▷ **Study Mate Supreme**

Gone are the days of crib notes and cheat sheets. With its massive database of information, ChatGPT is the only study mate you need. And remember that the more you chat in a thread, the more specific and tailored your research or study info will become!

▷ **Personal Coder**

The final way that you can start putting ChatGPT to work for you today, is as your own custom code generator. This is ideal for small businesses or individuals looking to create their own websites, without having to learn a whole bunch of coding language to do so, or pay someone an exorbitant amount to get it done. With ChatGPT, you have a personal coder in your pocket at any time. Just enter the prompt in regular English and it'll generate the code for it.

As you can see, there are a number of ways that you can start making use of ChatGPT today. But in order to get anything of value out of this lean, mean, deep-learning machine, you need to know how to give it the prompts it needs. If you want to get the right answer, you need to learn to ask the right questions, after all! Read on and discover how to speak to ChatGPT right, as we learn about the world of prompt engineering.

Prompt Engineering

Prompt engineering is the term we use to refer to the skill of entering prompts into ChatGPT in a way that "engineers" you the exact results that you were after. It's about crafting your inputs to perfection so that they help the LLM to pick up what you're typing down. This requires not only having an understanding of language models and how they function, but also needs quite a bit of creativity, as well as accuracy. And, like when communicating with a real person, context is key.

Why Is Prompt Engineering Important?

ChatGPT has changed the game in terms of AI that can generate text, images, or other media, but it's not perfect. One of the things that it severely lacks is exactly what we humans rely on to put what someone says into perspective: context. In order to make sense of what someone is saying to us, we use a lot more social cues than just the words that they say. We rely on their tone of voice, facial gestures, and body language, as well as the history of our relationship with the person speaking and how they fit into our lives. ChatGPT might have a heap of data, but it just doesn't have what it takes to bring context to the table on its own. Enter prompt engineering, where we humans take care of the context problem for our antisocial chatbot.

Through developing an understanding of prompt engineering, you'll be able to carefully structure your inputs, ensuring that ChatGPT has all the context it needs to be the dependable and useful digital PA of your dreams.

How Does It Work?

The big push into prompt engineering began with a paper published by computer scientist Ashish Vaswani and colleagues titled *Attention Is All You Need* (Vaswani et al., 2017). This paper introduced something called the attention mechanism, which was introduced to overcome the neural machine translation (NMT) problem. In simple terms, Vaswani and co. aimed to solve the problem of how to keep the responses received from generative AI accurate and focused, which was a particular problem when asking it for more complicated or lengthy responses. The attention mechanism enabled LLMs to focus on more than just the last prompt that it was given, allowing them to take into account the entire sequence of prompts given in a thread, and to weigh up the importance of different prompts (for example, putting more emphasis on accuracy than on producing anything that it can find on the topic).

The attention mechanism makes use of what peeps in the generative AI field call the transformer. Transformers are a group or "family" of machine learning architectures that allow LLMs like ChatGPT to determine the importance of the individual words in the prompts we enter. It does this using what's known as a self-attention mechanism. This mechanism weighs up your prompt according to three matrices: query, key, and value (Muñoz, 2020). Not only that, but it also weighs up its response to your prompt using these key elements too, so that it can give you more accurate results as the chat thread progresses. This is known as the "self-attention" mechanism of the AI. This all adds up (or is added up by the AI) to a chatbot that is capable of understanding some of the context surrounding the question, rather than just relying on the words in the prompt. Using the attention scores gained from the three matrices of query, key, and value, ChatGPT can measure how much it should focus on the individual words in a sequence based on what it knows about them, how you've phrased your previous prompts, and on where you placed the words in the sentence—as well as what words surround it (forming "chunks" of information). And this is where the new in-demand job in generative AI—prompt engineering—comes into play.

How Can You Use It?

Now, unless you want to try your hands at a new career of being a prompt engineer, chances are you don't need to know all of the technical math and code that goes into the matrices and architectures of the attention mechanism we mentioned above. In fact, all you need to get by with engineering your prompts with best success is a good understanding of the English language. As the former director of AI at Tesla, Andrej Karpathy once tweeted: "The hottest new programming language is English" (in Grant, 2023). In other words, you need to know how to word your request just right to make sure that the chatbot not only understands what info you're after, but also makes sure that you have compensated for the chatbot's lack of first-hand, real-world experience.

There are two main reasons why everyone interested in using chatbots and generative AI should make sure they understand the basics of prompt engineering. First of all, through learning what makes AI tick, you'll develop an in-depth understanding of the capabilities and limitations of ChatGPT and co. Secondly, it will make clear what skills you already possess that can be put to great use in engineering your prompts. Let's go over the five everyday skills that you can put to use while using generative AI.

Communication Skills and the Art of Giving Instructions

Do you have a skill listed on your CV as "great communicator" or something similar? If you do, it's time to put it to use when entering prompts into your chatbot! As anyone in a profession where you have to explain things to people knows, it's not easy to get the average person to follow instructions. Or rather, giving instructions to people in just the right way so that they can easily understand and implement them is a science bordering on an artform. Project managers and teachers, for example, have to continuously think: "How can I best phrase my instructions to get the results I'm after?" If you are in one of these professions, or a similar one, then you're in pretty good stead for communicating your prompt to ChatGPT in the way that, with a little trial and error, will get you the results you need.

If you're a parent, then you've also (hopefully) got these instruction-giving skills ready to transfer over into the digital world of chatbots. And, if the only time you have given instructions is to tell them to take off the tomato on your burger, don't worry! Just think back to your school days and the teacher that was the best at getting the most out of their class and use their style of instructions-giving, or to your parents and how they raised you to (once again, hopefully) know left from right and right from wrong. A takeaway tip is to keep your prompts as simple (in terms of language), as detailed (in terms of what you're looking for), and as action-oriented (in terms of instructions) as you can make them.

Professional Expertise

If you're looking to use ChatGPT to help you with your work-life, then you're in luck! Because you can then provide our powerful lil' chatbot with exactly what it's missing (and what you need to get the most out of it): real-world expertise. When we think of the profession that is prompt engineering, we're not thinking of a "Jack-of-all-trades" kind of person that can sit down and plug in the perfect prompt, no matter if the subject matter is health care or crypto currencies. It requires knowing the ins and outs of the industry, as well as the jargon and the lingo, in order to engineer the perfect prompt. Most job postings for prompt engineers are very clear that they're looking for those who have "industry-specific expertise" (Grant, 2023). While this means becoming a prompt engineer isn't as easy as you might have thought, it also means that you can engineer prompts yourself for your specific niche or industry. As we mentioned above, crafting powerful prompts requires feeding ChatGPT the real-world experience it's lacking.

Linguistic Prowess

If you've always had a fascination for languages, or at least remember what you learned in your high-school English classes, then you're in good stead to get the most out of chatbot prompts. Knowing your tenses, understanding the difference between active and passive voice, and having the vocabulary of a spelling bee champion has never been more useful in the world of AI. Having an in-depth understanding of the English language allows you to express yourself clearly, letting ChatGPT know exactly what you want to achieve from your prompt. And if you don't succeed with your first prompt, rework your sentence using your linguistic prowess until you have the perfect turn of phrase that the AI can't help but produce a similarly perfect response to. Remember: AI prompts don't run on some unknown coding language, they run on English prose.

Critical Thinking

The next skill that will do you well with ChatGPT and other generative AI, is some good ol' logic. Chatbots aren't close to perfect yet, and they still produce faulty results from time to time. In fact, as we'll see in the next section, some generative AI can straight-up hallucinate! When it does so, the chatbot spews out incorrect information and claims it as fact. It's then up to the prompt engineer to recognize the fake news and to ask the chatbot follow-up questions to deduce where the false information came from, and then work out how to get the correct answer. This is also why it's a good idea for the prompt engineer to have an in-depth understanding of the prompt's subject matter. And if you're using ChatGPT for something important, it's a good idea to fact-check the info it produces for you if you're not too sure about something.

Creative Thinking

Finally, a little bit of creativity can go a long way when it comes to engineering your prompts. While you should make sure your language is precise and your logic is sound, you shouldn't be afraid to mix things up and experiment with words, terms, and phrases in order to get the results you're after. If you're going to be using ChatGPT for more advanced searches or for complicated threads, then it may be a good idea to test out a variety of related prompts to see what works and what doesn't. Then, refine the instructions you feed into the chatbot based on these test prompts and watch the results you seek fly on in.

No AI Is Perfect

We've put together a few more pieces of the ChatGPT puzzle so far, but our image of this powerful LLM is not yet complete. To get the full picture, we not only need to know the strengths of chatbots, but their limitations and weaknesses too. Just like its creator, AI isn't perfect. As we mentioned in the section above, ChatGPT has been known to mess up its answers at times, to disseminate false information, or to even occasionally produce nonsensical responses. It's only as good as the data it's trained on after all, and that data was produced by us flawed humans. This doesn't make ChatGPT unusable for anything serious or complex, not by a long shot. It just means that you should make sure you know about generative AI's shortcomings, as well as how to compensate for them.

Main Limitations of ChatGPT

It's important to remember as we go through the main flaws of this revolutionary LLM that this is a brand-spanking-new breakthrough in technology, less than five years-old at the time of writing. So don't get down as we cover the limitations and weaknesses of ChatGPT—it's still more than useful and far from unusable. It's also many years away from its final update, so what's a flaw today could be turned into a strength tomorrow. With that disclaimer out of the way, let's now go through the top shortcomings faced by our maverick lil' chatbot.

No Internet Access

Believe it or not, although we may use the internet to access ChatGPT, the chatbot itself cannot connect to the internet. This means that while it can give real-time responses, it can't provide real-time info. So, if you planned to use ChatGPT to stay up to date with the latest weather reports, trading stats, or news stories (or to write them for you), I've got some bad news for you. This is because, unlike Google, ChatGPT is not a search engine; it's a language processing program. Watch this space though, as ChatGPT is teaming up with the likes of Microsoft's Bing to overcome this limitation and make our lil' chatbot bigger and better than ever before. Talk about a "probletunity."

Limited Knowledge and Shallow Responses

With its 570 gigs of data, it may seem like ChatGPT has all the info on the internet at its disposal, ready to pull from whenever needed. But the truth is that, when compared to a professional in a certain field, the chatbot comes up second-best in terms of knowledge and the depth of its responses. While it will respond to pretty much any prompt you enter with related information, it's been found that the amount of detail in these responses can range from short, incomplete summaries to long answers loaded with lots of fluff (i.e., irrelevant information). An example of this is to ask ChatGPT to explain our use of mobile phones. Rather than providing a full rundown of this complicated technology and its history of use, the chatbot will respond with a short answer and won't really want to elaborate on it when asked to. It's then up to the user to get creative with their prompt to engineer it in a way that does get the response they're after.

Emotionless, Expressionless Writing

If you had to grade ChatGPT on the creativity of its responses, you'd realize very quickly just how limited its uses can be for writing prose and poetry. Robots are not renowned for being the most in-touch with their emotions, and our antisocial chatbot is no exception. The answers it gives will always be in a formal tone using direct, straightforward language and sentence structure. And so, what it produces can come across as emotionless, with a dire lack of expressive language (something we humans pride ourselves on). When it comes to writing poetry, for example, ChatGPT might use the vocabulary and grammar of a university graduate, but it still has the emotional understanding of a machine. And so the poem it produces for you will be flatter, drier, and less emotive or expressive than one written by a fifth-grader.

Struggles With Complicated Math

While machines aren't renowned for their poetry writing skills, they are known to be excellent mathematicians. But ChatGPT is not the master mathematician that you may think. It can do the simple stuff of adding, subtracting, multiplying, and dividing at the drop of a hat, but when asked to solve more complicated equations that require a number of different mathematical operations, the chatbot will often produce inaccurate results, or even throw in the towel completely.

Unable to Multitask Effectively

Even though ChatGPT can hold onto loads of information and recall it pretty much instantly in order to answer your prompt, it doesn't do too well with handling multiple tasks at once. This is because generative AI struggles to prioritize which task is more important than the others, decreasing the accuracy of its answers as you add more tasks for it to compute. To get the most out of ChatGPT, give it one thing to focus on at a time.

Hidden Biases

A generative AI is only as good as the dataset on which it was created. If the data it is fed contains biased or prejudiced information, then these become the biases and prejudices the chatbot generates in its responses too. This is not to say that ChatGPT is racist or sexist, just that the internet is not renowned for being free of such things, and it's the internet that provided the dataset used to build ChatGPT. Add to this its lack of emotional intelligence and human common sense, as well as its struggle to understand context, and we can see why some responses generated by ChatGPT have been found to be biased or even discriminatory (unintentionally, of course).

Limited Skills With Long-Form Content

As we mentioned earlier, if you're expecting a chatbot to write the next *New York Times* bestseller, I've got some bad news for you. In fact, at present, it seems that ChatGPT has quite a bit of difficulty in producing well-structured, engaging, or even comprehensible long-form content. It can generate grammatically correct and coherent sentences, but this degrades in quality, accuracy, and coherency as we reach the paragraph level, and even more so as you ask it to produce longer form essays and stories. At the moment, the chatbot struggles quite a lot with narrative writing, and as such, is best used for shorter pieces like summary articles, bullet point lists, or short descriptions and explanations.

As we can see, ChatGPT still has a long way to go until it can be used for anything and everything. Remember that this poster child of AI chatbots is still in its teething stages, and there will be many more updates and upgrades to come. Even with its shortcomings, some of the largest companies and richest people in the world are jumping on the ChatGPT bandwagon. I have too, and so should you!

We've now learned a whole heap about how large language models work, as well as what makes them tick and where their artificial limits lie. Now it's time to move on fully from the theory to the practical as we look at a number of real-life applications for ChatGPT. Turn the page to chapter three as we learn about how to turn this nifty lil' chatbot into your very own personal butler.

Chapter 3
Your Personal Butler

If you're like me, I'm sure there's been more than a time or two in your life when you've thought to yourself: "Wouldn't it be great if I had a personal assistant to take care of all this boring admin work." Well, I've got some great news for us, because ChatGPT is the prime virtual assistant of the modern age! Just like Batman has Alfred Pennyworth, you too can have your very own personal butler.

In many ways, ChatGPT is better than an in-person PA. First of all, you can get hold of the chatbot any time, anywhere. It never sleeps, never has to take lunch breaks, never goes on holiday, will never complain of being overworked, and, best of all, won't ever ask you for a raise. In fact, this powerful virtual PA comes without any price tag attached—all it costs is some time learning how to use it right. And that's exactly what we're going to cover in this chapter!

Becoming the Butler

The idea of a virtual assistant or digital PA is not a new concept. In fact, it's something that most companies use nowadays as the first line of contact between customer and business. There are also the personal virtual assistants of Siri, Alexa, Google Assistant, and Microsoft Cortana. In this section, we're going to go over how ChatGPT, the next great development in digital assistance, has become the perfect Alfred to our Batman, both for personal and professional life.

Trusting in Your Intelligent Virtual Assistant

One of the biggest attractions of using generative AI and deep learning models is to take over a lot of the more boring, administrative and research-based tasks that we come across in our personal and professional lives. These tasks can result in us spending a significant amount of time in our day stuck in the world of admin, without ever getting to what was meant to be the main focus of our day. Planning and preparation, researching and organizing; these types of tasks take us humans a long time to complete (especially if we don't really want to do them), but deep learning models like ChatGPT can complete them quicker than it took us to engineer and enter in our prompt.

But what makes ChatGPT the perfect PA? Well, first of all, its natural language processing (NLP) or natural language understanding (NLU) algorithm means that it can not only understand and reply using humanesque language, but also make judgements based on the history of the "conversation" you're having with it. As you shall see later on in this section, this gives ChatGPT a unique set of skills that makes it perfect for the job of a PA. Before we get there, let's go over the reasons why ChatGPT makes such a supreme intelligent virtual assistant.

Contextual Awareness

While it may not be able to pick up on the same kinds of context we humans can, ChatGPT picks up a lot more of it than the other digital assistants out there do. This is because it's able to keep the other prompts in a conversation thread in mind, meaning that the more you chat to it, the better it becomes at picking up your intent, and the more accurately it will complete the task that you set it.

Episodic Memory

In order to keep in mind the previous prompts in your thread, ChatGPT uses its episodic memory. This means that it is able to remember past "events," memorize the conversation's history, and recall it as and when needed further down the line in the thread.

Next Intent Prediction

ChatGPT doesn't only use its episodic memory to help it with being more contextually aware, but also to predict the future! Well, not quite, but it can use the data it gets from your current conversation or prompt to try and predict what your next prompt is going to be, or what the next conversation topic could be about. This helps it to further tailor the information that it provides you with in real time.

Self-Learning

The next thing that makes ChatGPT the perfect PA is its self-learning abilities. This means that it not only remembers previous conversations and uses them to become better at context and prediction, but it actually *learns* from the conversations you have with it too. This means that ChatGPT can become the most trainable PA you could ever have!

Plug Into Existing Communication Channels

Using ChatGPT doesn't mean that you have to leave behind other communication channels. In fact, you can integrate the artificially intelligent assistant into your existing communication channels, such as Skype, Microsoft Teams, and even Facebook Messenger and Telegram. To do this, you just have to add the chatbot as a virtual team member on these platforms.

Graph Creator

Our intelligent virtual assistant isn't only good at the written form either. It's also a pretty darn talented graph generator. So, if you're looking for a more visual way of presenting your data, look no further than ChatGPT! It can interpret the info you give it, identify the key factors, and turn them into easy-to-understand graphs. Some of the ways ChatGPT can visualize your data are as bar, line, or pie graphs, histograms, or scatter plots.

Polyglot Pro

For all intents and purposes, ChatGPT can be considered one of the best polyglots on the planet. A polyglot is someone who knows and is able to use multiple languages. While English is ChatGPT's first and most fluent language (as it makes up the majority of the dataset it was trained on), ChatGPT can understand and respond in over 90 different languages. Other languages that the chatbot is good at communicating in are Spanish, French, German, and Mandarin Chinese (as these are the other languages most prominently found in its training data).

Executive PA ChatGPT in Action

Virtual assistants already follow us around every day, whether we make use of them or not. These digital PAs are programmed to make our lives easier in very specific ways and are designed with the purpose of providing us tech users with a simple and efficient means to "chat" and interact with our gadgets and gizmos. There are loads of uses for virtual assistants, from adding tasks to our calendar, checking flight reservations, writing text messages for us, or even running and controlling smart-home devices, filling the role of a digital butler. So, if these digital PAs have been around for a while (more than a decade for Siri and Alexa) and already fill a wide variety of different administrative, assistance, and automation positions, how is the large language model of ChatGPT any different?

Well, first of all, the mass amount of data that LLMs are trained on, and their ability to generate human-like sentences in real time, puts them ahead of the other applicants for becoming your perfect virtual assistant. To test out just how perfectly ChatGPT could work as your one-stop-shop digital PA, *New*

York Time's lead consumer technology writer and Tech Fix columnist Brian Chen decided to put the chatbot to the test. He devised a list of different tasks that would be asked of a virtual assistant (whether human or AI), including helping him to prepare for a meeting, summarize the meeting notes, plan business trips and create itineraries, and manage his calendar, including booking meetings and rescheduling some appointments.

He then told the chatbot that he was the chief executive of a company called "Artificially Intelligent" and that it was his executive assistant. Then, he set ChatGPT to work as his PA for the day.

Meeting Prep

The first thing Chen asked the chatbot to do was to help him prepare for a meeting with a potential investor. He chose Scott Forstall, the former Apple executive whose work history is handily made available to the general public (and forms part of ChatGPT's dataset). Chen asked his digital PA to do a background check on the guy and to help write up some talking points that would help to persuade Forstall to invest in his start-up.

And according to Chen, "ChatGPT did the job with aplomb" (Chen, 2023). It not only summarized the former Apple executive's work history and education, but also provided helpful strategies on how to best approach Forstall, win him over, and ensure that he invests. This is an excerpt of the advice executive assistant ChatGPT gave its boss:

"Showcase how your start-up combines A.I. with other fields, such as cognitive psychology, linguistics or neuroscience, to create innovative solutions. This interdisciplinary approach may resonate with Scott, given his academic background in Symbolic Systems" (Chen, 2023).

When Chen shared ChatGPT's recommended pitching points with Scott Forstall, the former Apple executive had this to say:

"Overall, ChatGPT provides a compelling road map on how you could build a persuasive customized pitch deck specifically targeting me. Now that you have my attention, what exactly is your A.I. start-up?" (Chen, 2023).

Meeting Notes

Next up, Chen asked his nifty new executive assistant to summarize the notes from an internal meeting that his fictional AI startup had. The meeting topic? "A public relations crisis in which users of my A.I. start-up's technology believed that the bot had become sentient" (Chen, 2023). Got to love Chen's sense of humor, although such things are lost on our emotionless robot. The "meeting" was between three people—Chen, Karen, the chief technology officer, and Henry, the chief communications officer—trying to do damage control and to put out a statement explaining to the public that their AI had, in fact, *not* become self-aware.

ChatGPT proved to be the perfect PA once again, producing a detailed memo that captured attendance and the main points of the discussion. It then went on to create an action plan with roles for each attendee. It decided Henry, as chief communications officer, would craft the statement, Karen and Chen would review it, and once they'd accepted it, Henry would release the statement to the public the following morning.

Trip Planning

Two tests passed with flying colors. Chen then put ChatGPT through the third: Planning an itinerary for a business trip to Taipei, Taiwan. He tasked his assistant to pick a hotel near the city center, allowing enough time in Taipei before the meeting to accommodate for jet lag. Chen also requested places to eat and for the itinerary to include a weekend in the city before returning home. Once again, ChatGPT proved the perfect personal assistant, selecting a good location in the city center and suggesting some good places to eat. It also set a thoughtful itinerary of arriving on a Sunday, taking Monday off to account for jet lag, and to have the business meeting on Tuesday.

Calendar Setting

The final task that Chen set for his potential PA was the one that it did worst in: Setting and checking his calendar. Unfortunately, this is also one of the main jobs that an executive assistant does, and does put a bit of a downer on the whole experiment. But there is a silver lining, as it's well-known why ChatGPT can't set your calendar for you, and there are serious works underway to ensure that it can in the future. Before we get to the solution, let's go over the task Chen set for his virtual assistant, and why exactly it didn't work out so well.

Chen told the chatbot that he needed to go to the dentist, and asked it to check his calendar for him and find a time slot in his busy schedule that could be used for the appointment. But ChatGPT was unable to do this for him because, at present, it isn't capable of accessing people's calendars (remember what we said earlier about generative AI not actually being able to access the real-time internet). But fear not, as OpenAI is actively working to solve this pitfall by teaming up with third-party service companies such as Expedia, Instacart, and OpenTable. Through these partnerships, ChatGPT will be able to access your internet via a plug-in. This is just the in-between of OpenAI's true goal in the field of calendar setting, which is to get ChatGPT working directly with calendar apps (Chen, 2023).

Making NLU Work for You

ChatGPT is a large-language model that uses natural language processing and its deep learning database to produce humanesque conversations responding to prompts that the user (aka you) enters into it. One of the key things that makes this possible is ChatGPT's ability to understand human language. Known as its natural language understanding (NLU) capability, this is one of the things that makes it such a revolutionary technology, and is the next way you can begin leveraging the chatbot as your virtual PA.

While the LLM should find it pretty easy to understand almost all kinds of text you give it, it's still important to remember that the onus is on you as the prompt engineer to ensure that ChatGPT understands what you mean and what you're after. Remember that generative AI is in no way perfect, and has been known to "hallucinate" and spew out incorrect information. It does this when it doesn't fully understand the context of your prompt, and thus generates text that falls outside of your parameters (including providing you with incorrect information and then claiming it as fact). To stop this from happening, you need to make sure that your prompt explicitly mentions that you want it to only use the info you provide it with in the prompt and nothing else. This might limit the research uses of ChatGPT, but ensures that the results you get from it are, well, true. When using ChatGPT, providing context is key.

Customer Service

The first thing ChatGPT can do is serve as your customer liaison. As we've mentioned before, generative AI has served as the first line between the customer and business for a while now. But this kind of software was initially quite pricey and generally only feasible for larger companies to use. ChatGPT has leveled the playing field by being better than anything that came before.

Powered by its deep learning model, the chatbot can understand customer inquiries and respond to them in a conversational, humanesque manner. It can also help you to automate a lot of the customer service tasks that plague the solopreneur or lean start-up. These include providing answers to questions frequently asked by customers, thanking the customer for making a purchase, or signing up to your newsletter. This can save time and money spent on customer service in the early days of starting your company, or if you are a solo operation.

Business Analysis and Market Research

Not only can ChatGPT help you to automate a lot of general customer service tasks, but it can also analyze the conversations it has with your customers, and along with the info it has in its dataset, use this to identify customer trends. This will allow you to develop a better idea of who your customer is, and will also help you to form a plan of action for what you can do to make their experience with your company even better.

Not only that, but this lil' chatbot of ours is also the perfect business coach, providing good advice and also taking care of that time-consuming task of conducting market research. Finally, ChatGPT has the nifty skill of analyzing data to "predict" what could happen in the future. This includes predicting future market trends and changes in customer behavior. It can also present all this information using charts, graphs, and other types of visual aids. Talk about handy!

Process Modeling

Process modeling is about depicting the different steps someone (or a team) needs to complete to achieve a certain goal. This is generally done in a flowchart style that presents the steps in a clear and visually appealing way. It's also a great way to capture information in your pitching presentation or business plan, if you're looking to start your own business. ChatGPT can advise you on the best process models to use for the specific task you're trying to complete or goal you're trying to achieve. You can also ask ChatGPT to ask you clarifying questions about your process model and help you work on describing the different steps of the process based on its database of similar models. This allows you to revise and edit your process model as you go, whether it be a new dieting plan, exercise routine, pitch deck, or marketing campaign. Whatever project you're looking to undertake, ChatGPT can be your perfect program manager!

Using ChatGPT for Project Management

Speaking of ChatGPT being your virtual project manager, let's dive into a bit more detail on that. As anyone who's tried to run a project before knows, it's damn hard work. Most of us have a hard enough time managing ourselves, let alone taking on any other kinds of projects. It takes a lot of careful planning, and if your team is larger than just you, you're also going to need to work out a lot of logistics in terms of coordination and communication. Instead of going gray trying to do this yourself, outsource the grunt work to ChatGPT. As we saw above, ChatGPT can help you to perfect your process models. It can also help you with brainstorming by generating lists of ideas or important details related to a specific topic. Besides assisting with the early planning stages of a project, there's also a heap more that our virtual assistant supreme can help you with.

Project Planning

The first thing that ChatGPT is great at is helping you to create plans for your various projects. It can take the information you give it, evaluate it, provide recommendations, and even ask you questions such as: "What is your projected timeline for completing your task?" or "What is the first milestone for your project?" If you don't know the answer, then turn the tables and ask the question back at ChatGPT, such as: "What key milestones should be included in a project schedule for X?" Finally, ChatGPT can help you to work out the ideal project schedule based on your task, timeline, and budget.

Team Collaboration

Working with someone else, or in a team, has never been easier than it is today, especially if you employ ChatGPT as your project managing assistant. The nifty lil' chatbot can function as a virtual team member, ready to record notes, and to answer any questions that pop up in relation to data or info. All you have to do is integrate ChatGPT into whatever team communication platform you use, and presto! You have the power of the virtual PA supreme sitting in on each and every meeting and team chat you have. It can then take over the task of monitoring the progress of tasks and ensure that everyone is on the same page, so to speak.

Risk Assessment

ChatGPT is great at examining data, identifying trends, and even giving some insightful views (depending on the prompts you engineer for it). This makes it a great tool to use for assessing and mitigating risk in the projects that you manage. It can help you to analyze project data, as well as compile highlight summaries of historical trends, or research external factors that could influence your project and hinder its process. It can also give feedback on your project model, mitigating potential risks before they arise.

An example of this in action would be asking ChatGPT what the potential risks to a project are. You could then take this a step further by asking how it would go about mitigating the identified risks. The chatbot would then generate insights on how to mitigate or reduce the risks faced with a particular project. Remember to enter the risks individually into your prompts in order to get the most accurate answers from your new virtual PA.

Decision-Making

As anyone who's ever dipped their toes into the waters of project management knows, decision-making is never as clear-cut as an easy "yes" or "no." There are always a number of factors to weigh up before a final decision is reached. ChatGPT can help by giving you an outsider's analysis; an objective perspective, if you will. You can either ask your virtual PA to provide you with facts and figures related to the decision you have to make, or to place the information into graphs. You can also ask it to ask you questions related to the decision. Examples of the questions it could produce are: "What are the pros of each approach and what are their cons?" or "What implications could arise from your decision to choose X and not Y?"

Knowledge Management

One of the keys to success with any project, no matter how big or small, is to accurately store and effectively manage the information and documentation for it. Rather than wasting crucial time doing this manually, ChatGPT can help you to automate the organization of said data and knowledge, ensuring that it's ready to retrieve at a moment's notice. It can also provide research on the best knowledge management models to use for your specific project, and ask pertinent questions related to the project based on the chatbot's massive repository of project management knowledge and the historical data of the project.

And there you have it! A step-by-step guide on how to use ChatGPT as your project management assistant supreme. Remember that our virtual assistant can help you complete your project, no matter how big or small, whether personal or professional. ChatGPT is there, come rain or shine, 24/7, 365, ready and waiting to help you succeed, achieve your goals, and start living the life of your dreams. And, if you don't quite know how to make your dreams reality just yet, ask ChatGPT what the best way to manage such a project would be and see what results you get. Remember, what you get out is what you put in, so make sure to engineer your prompts as carefully as an actual engineer would their blueprints.

ChatGPT as a Content Creator's Assistant

In this final section on how to use ChatGPT as your artificially intelligent PA, we're going to look at how it can assist you with the more creative side of things, such as creating content for social media, writing blogs, and so on. You can use ChatGPT to help you create and organize content for your own social media profiles, or you can use it to help you start a business where you create content for other people too. It's important to note that ChatGPT isn't taking away the jobs of writers and content creators; it's actually making our lives so much easier, and can help us to start earning more money too!

Social Media Content Creator

One of the most time consuming things when first starting your own business, or trying to gain traction as a creative, is to plan out your social media campaigns. Generally, we wait until the first available opportunity to hand over the running of our various social platforms to a social media manager. But no longer do we have to wait until making money to save time on content creation; just make use of the virtual social media manager that is ChatGPT. Our chatbot can help you research possible content for your niche, generate short-form copy (with human editing still needed), and even help you to make a social media calendar. And, once you get used to using ChatGPT to help create and manage your social media, you can start doing it for other people too, creating a side-hustle income stream.

Blog Writer

Besides creating content for social media, ChatGPT can also be a great blog-writing assistant. It can do pretty much all of the research side for you, all you have to do is engineer the right prompt. It's also great at creating outlines, or the bare bones of a blog for you to write or edit up yourself. And, if you can use ChatGPT to write blogs for yourself, you can also use it to write blogs for other people, offering it as a service alongside social media content creation!

SEO and Hashtag Expert

Added to ChatGPT's skills in content creation, copywriting, and blog writing is its expertise in search engine optimization and hashtags. SEO involves making your blogs or website more palatable (or findable) by search engines such as Google and Bing by including popular and frequently searched keywords. Hashtags work in a similar way on social media, categorizing and allowing your content to show up in people's feeds should they search for your hashtag, or if they regularly view content with similar hashtags. All you have to do is enter a prompt like: "Create ten hashtags I can use on Instagram about X," or "Make a list of the fifteen most popular SEO keywords related to Y."

Pitch Writer Pro

The final way that ChatGPT can serve as your content creating virtual assistant is by helping you to research and write business and PR pitches. Since the LLM has loads of data on pitching, it's the prime aid for helping you write yours, too! You can also use ChatGPT to generate a pitch for you, but make sure to give it enough context in your prompt first, and to do some human editing after.

Prompts to Use for ChatGPT

So far in this chapter, we've learned how you can use ChatGPT as the ultimate virtual assistant. It can help you research almost any topic under the sun, streamline your workflow, automate your schedule, or of course, generate a whole bunch of content on a wide array of subject matter. But, as we mentioned before, our artificially intelligent assistant does have its limits, and one of those is that ChatGPT only produces results as good as the prompt that you enter into it.

You now know the theory behind prompt engineering, and now's the time to start putting it to practice. It's time to go over some examples of the types of prompts you can type into ChatGPT that are perfectly engineered to generate you some prime content. Whether you're an entrepreneur, researcher, or creative; we've got you covered with a list of prompts for you to choose from. Let's get our prompt on (Kapoor, 2023)!

Prompts for Entrepreneurs

- Write a business proposal for launching X products, giving detailed analysis of the market demand and market saturation.
- Generate the plan for a social media campaign optimized for showcasing company culture.
- Create a list of the optimum keywords related to X product/service.
- Write a blog post on X event aimed at achieving Y result.
- Create a list of potential investors interested in the X industry.

Prompts for Researchers

- Generate a study schedule for the next two weeks focused on X number of subjects with Y amount of breaks in a day.
- Teach me about X, making sure to include Y.
- Generate a summary of all the information on X between the following dates.
- Create a list of potential topics for X type of essay/research topic.
- Write a detailed essay on X, using basic English and explaining it like you would to an eight-year-old.

Prompts for Creatives/Freelancers

- Create a detailed plan for monetizing X artform, focusing on social media and online platforms.
- Provide a step-by-step tutorial on how to set up an art workshop.
- Generate a list of the best tools and materials to use for X.
- Write a detailed summary of how to apply for an artist grant or fellowship at X.
- Compile a list of the top-rated resources for creatives/freelancers, including books, courses, podcasts, and YouTube videos.

Prompts for Writers

- Generate a detailed plan for self-publishing X type of book aimed at Y audience.
- Compile a guide for writing compelling characters.
- Produce an outline for a [number of words] book on X topic aimed at Y audience.
- Develop a detailed checklist for writing a novel, including planning, writing the first draft, and editing.
- Write an article summarizing the most effective ways to craft an opening line for a novel.

"Act As" Prompts

- Act as a professional editor specializing in nonfiction books. Read the introduction to my book on mastering AI conversations and provide constructive feedback.
- Act as my social media manager. Formulate a comprehensive strategy for marketing my product/service on all popular social media platforms.
- Act as a business strategist. Develop a detailed and actionable business strategy for launching a startup in the X industry.
- Act as a travel agent. Create a detailed itinerary for a 10 day business trip to X destination, including popular activities to do and places to eat on the weekends.
- Act as a teacher. Create a detailed lesson plan for teaching X topic to Y group of people (age and/or level).

Voila! A list of 25 actionable prompts for you to use for a variety of different situations and professions. If this list didn't have the type of prompt that you were after, feel free to re-engineer them, tweaking them until they get you the type of response you're after from your nifty new virtual PA. As you can see, ChatGPT not only answers prompts, but can also perform "role-play" exercises with you, taking on the perspective of a wide variety of professions to help give you feedback, ask compelling questions, or even generate content from different professional perspectives. Now, tell me that isn't a pretty cool skill for a PA to have.

Over the next few chapters, we'll carry on defining the different roles that ChatGPT can take on to help you in both your personal and professional life. So far, we've seen that OpenAI's chatbot makes a super artificially intelligent assistant. But, as we discovered in the "act as" prompts, the LLM can do way more than a human PA ever could: It can fill the role of many other professions too. If having a virtual assistant isn't quite your thing, what about having your very own personal counselor, ready and waiting with a listening ear and expert advice, whenever and wherever you need it? Flip on through to the next chapter as we look into the softer side of ChatGPT and how it can function as your very own therapeutic assistant-on-demand.

Chapter 4
Therapy on Demand

In the tech-obsessed busyness that is the world of today, therapy is not only more needed than ever before, but is more easily accessible than ever before too. In fact, in the digital age, therapy can be just a text message away.

The fast pace at which the modern world works can put a lot of stress on us hairless monkeys. There is so much to do in the average day that most of us rarely get through everything on our "to-do" list, and the tasks just keep on piling up. This can leave us feeling tired, worn out, burnt-out, or even downright depressed. To stop this from happening, we need to learn how to delegate tasks and de-stress from the day. In the previous chapter, we saw how ChatGPT can serve as your ultimate virtual assistant, taking over much of the grunt work from your day, streamlining your workflow, and allowing you to delegate a hefty chunk of your to-do list over to it (or at the very least, get it to help you with it).

In this chapter, we're going to learn how our deep learning chatbot can go even further; helping you de-stress from daily life, providing you with a listening ear, and offering soothing, expert advice that can help you clear the storm clouds away and keep a steady eye on the silver linings. Now, it's important to remember that ChatGPT is not a licensed therapist, and while it's an uber-helpful tool, it is no substitute for professional mental health care. That being said, OpenAI's LLM can provide you with sound conversational support and help you cope with stress, anxiety, and loneliness.

We'll begin this therapeutic chapter with a chat about why taking care of your mental health is so important in today's fast-paced and stress-prone world, before outlining digital solutions for mental health support. Once that's done, it's time to cover that all-important question: Can AI really care? Finally, we'll provide you with all the tips, tricks, and insider info on how to get the most out of ChatGPT as your therapist on demand, as well as give you a list of primely engineered prompts to get you started. It's time to upgrade your ChatGPT skills once more as you turn it into both your virtual assistant and personal counselor!

Mind Matters

Mental health has become one of the catchphrases of the modern age, and with good reason. According to studies from the National Institute of Mental Health, an average of one in five adults presently live with moderate to severe mental health conditions (Girolimon, 2022). Other statistics released by the

Centers for Disease Control and Prevention show that more than half of Americans will experience and be diagnosed with some form of mental health condition at some point in their lives (CDCP, 2023). But what exactly is being mentally healthy (or unhealthy) all about?

Mental Health Explained

The best way to think of mental health is as the cross-section between our psychological, emotional, and social well-being. This means that our mental health is responsible for the way that we think, act, and feel on a daily basis. It also plays a role in our ability to make sound decisions, deal with stress, and our relationships with others. In other words, our mental health determines whether we see that proverbial glass of water as half empty or half full. If we want to be productive at work and effective at whatever we set our minds to doing, then we need to keep on top of our mental health.

There are many different ways that we can ensure we are mentally healthy and ready to take on whatever the world has to throw at us. This includes getting enough exercise, having a balanced diet, keeping a regular sleep schedule, and making sure to get out on the social scene every now and again. And, if you think keeping on top of any of those is beyond you, I've got some good news: ChatGPT can help you do exactly that!

Challenges to Accessing Mental Health

While keeping on top of your mental health should be a priority for all, it's not easy for all to access it. There are various reasons for this, and not all of them are fair. But that's life for you. In an ideal world, everyone would have access to their very own mental health practitioner or therapist (should they require one) to help them deal with the stresses and strains of being a human in the crazily complicated world we've built for ourselves. I'd like to think that ChatGPT is a step in the right direction for turning this ideal world into reality. We'll cover exactly how ChatGPT can help you improve your mental health in the next section. For now, let's lay the basework by covering the main reasons why people struggle to gain access to mental health care.

Financial Barriers

The first reason why many people don't get the mental health care they need is because of the price tag attached to getting it. Mental health issues affect everyone, from rich to poor, but the rich are at least able to afford to get the help they need. Those less well-off financially not only don't have the money to pay for help and treatment, but they also encounter many more of the stresses and strains, worries and woes in their daily life that exacerbate mental health problems. Harvard University's National Comorbidity Survey found that 47% of those that responded by saying they had some form of mental health issue also said that they couldn't afford to get help, but that they would seek help if they could (Adracare, 2021).

Time Restraints

The next thing keeping people from seeking out mental health care is the amount of time it takes waiting to see a mental health professional. As we mentioned earlier in this chapter, almost half of people suffer from some form of mental health problem at some point in their lives. This means that therapists and psychiatrists are often fully booked with a waiting list that could be two weeks or even longer. Because of the amount of people needing their help, most mental health professionals operate by a system of urgency, prioritizing those that have more pronounced or serious mental health problems. This means that those considered to have less time-sensitive mental health issues are often pushed to the back of the queue, making them less likely to seek help or causing their mental well-being to deteriorate even more.

Access Issues

There are also accessibility issues attached to seeking out mental health care. In poorer communities where the stresses and strains of life are at their harshest, there is generally a shortage of mental health services available. This isn't because all the therapists and psychiatrists flock to the rich areas, but because there is a severe lack of trained healthcare professionals out there. In fact, according to the Health Resources and Services Administration, nearly half of Americans live in areas considered to be "federally designated Mental Health Professional Shortage Areas" (Social Solutions, 2022). This makes the shortage of mental health professionals more severe than any other medical or healthcare professional.

Lack of Mental Health Awareness

The next common barrier preventing people from getting the help they need for their mental health is the lack of education and awareness out there about it. As we've mentioned, mental health is one of the catchwords of the modern age. But it hasn't always been that way. In fact, until pretty recently, mental health issues were by-and-large ignored, even by the people that suffered from them! When we hurt ourselves or get sick, there are usually physical signs and symptoms that make it clear we're not doing so great. It also shows to other people, who can encourage the injured or ill person to get help. Mental health issues, on the other hand, can be quite tricky to recognize. The symptoms of such problems are often very subtle and can often be glossed over as being "just who the person is," or as an "attitude problem." Worst of all, the person suffering from the mental health problem can convince themselves that it's just who they are, or that it's normal to feel the mentally drained and slightly deranged way they do. The more aware people become of the different mental disorders out there, as well as their clinical symptoms, the more likely they are to realize that the way they feel doesn't have to be the status quo and can improve. But, without more easily accessible (and understandable) information on mental health awareness to educate them on their condition, many people are not going to seek out help or treatment.

Social Stigmas

The final major challenge hindering people from getting the mental health care they need is that there seems to be a lingering stigma attached to seeking help for such things. As we mentioned above, in the recent past, it was common practice for many to straight-up ignore the mental health issues of themselves and others. We humans are a proud species and can be very slow to seek out or accept help from others. This can lead people to feel that they are somehow letting themselves or others down when seeking help with their mental well-being. People seem to feel like they will be discriminated against if they acknowledge they may have a mental health issue, and that their family or friends will avoid them if they seek out help or treatment for it. These thoughts are found in all strata of society, from the individual psyche to cultural beliefs, from personal to professional life. "How can we solve something so ingrained in our minds?" you may ask. Well, my friend, it all begins with becoming more educated as to what mental well-being is all about, and at least at the beginning, providing a way to seek out help discreetly for those that fear discrimination. ChatGPT can help us achieve both of these goals, and slowly but surely, to overcome these wrongly held public perceptions surrounding mental health. Best of all, it's already doing so. But more on that in a bit.

The Rise of Digital Solutions for Mental Health Support

In the world of today, technological advancements and automatization are the name of the game. No matter what sector you work in, the people in charge are doing their damndest to incorporate tech into every level they can. Technology is the new frontier of the world, and is transforming the way we interact with the world around us, whether it be in our personal or professional lives. And the mental health sector is no different.

Digital mental health solutions had been improving at a pretty standard rate until COVID-19 hit, and then it began to increase exponentially. Since the pandemic, digital solutions to mental health support have been playing more and more of a key role in the overall mental health care sector. It's not only the carry-over from the pandemic that's leading the digitalization of mental health care, but also a mass increase in people seeking mental health support and resources. As we mentioned earlier in this chapter, mental health is a catchphrase in the world of today, but historically, there have been major challenges for certain segments of the population to gain access to the mental health care landscape. This is rapidly changing, and digital solutions in mental health care are leading this revolutionary drive to make mental health care available for anyone and everyone.

And if you're one of those die-hards that believes there's no way digital mental healthcare solutions can measure up to visiting an actual human therapist, I've got news for you: There's a growing body of research that says it can be just as effective (WEconnect, 2023). In fact, the ease of use, flexibility of appointments, and anonymous nature means that many who normally wouldn't seek help *are* through the digital platforms. For these people, the digital solution to their problem is the preferred one, because otherwise they never would have sought help for their problem in the first place.

Before coronavirus shut down our world, it was estimated that around 25% of the world's population suffered from depression

(Heeg, 2021). And experts in the field of mental health say this percentage rose dramatically during the pandemic. According to a study by the Organisation for Economic Co-operation and Development (OECD), "From March 2020 onwards, prevalence of anxiety and depression increased and in some countries even doubled" (OECD, 2021). A key thing to note in that quote is the use of the word "onwards." That means it's still ongoing, because you can't just ignore a mental health problem or wish it away. Just like a physical health problem, if you don't seek help for that proverbial lump in your mind, it's not going to go away. In fact, it's probably going to get bigger, and like cancer, spread more and more throughout your mentality and mindset. But don't worry, because digital mental healthcare solutions have you covered and there's no need to wait until you have the money for it, or for when they have the time to see you; you can jump on your phone or computer and get help, right now! Not saying you need to, obviously, but it is quite a revolutionary thing to be able to do, and we should start viewing it like that. The modern world is a stressful place with a lot of uncertainty. Why shouldn't we all have access to our own personal digital therapist to help us keep our mental and emotional wellbeing at prime levels; helping us to not sink or swim, but ride the wave of modern life and all that it has to offer?

Can AI Really Care?

As we saw in the section above, there has been a massive rise in the use of digital tools in the mental healthcare sector. This has helped to democratize mental health support, making it available to everyone. And, if COVID-19 took digital therapy a few steps forward, the invention of LLMs like ChatGPT have exponentialized that, carrying online mental healthcare forward in leaps and bounds while simultaneously making it even more accessible to anyone who needs it, but who can't afford to go the traditional therapeutic route.

Now, it's important to remember what we said at the outset of this here chapter: ChatGPT isn't a licensed therapist and cannot be used in place of actual therapy when it comes to serious mental health issues. But for less pronounced mental healthcare support, or as a first line of contact, it's as good (if not better than) as going the traditional face-to-face way. What ChatGPT excels at is providing conversational therapy and support that can help us deal with the stress, anxiety, loneliness, and other negative emotional states that affect our mental health. "But isn't ChatGPT antisocial and emotionally disconnected?" I hear you ask. While it is true that our chatbot generally struggles to determine context and pick up on emotional cues, this changes once you learn how to engineer your prompts to compensate for these kinds of factors.

The Benefits of an AI Therapist

Once you've got the hang of engineering your prompts with a therapeutic twist, ChatGPT can pretty accurately simulate empathetic responses and the active listening skills employed by therapists and psychiatrists. It can also provide you with advice on how to make a treatment program that will get you back to your mental A game in no time flat. Let's go through some examples of how exactly ChatGPT can serve as your own personal virtual therapist-on-demand.

Personalized Support

The first thing that makes ChatGPT a good virtual therapist is its ability to be tailored to your specific needs. As an LLM, the chatbot can take the prompt you gave it expressing your mental health concern and determine whether you're feeling sad, stressed, anxious, or depressed. It can then provide responses specifically dealing with your concerns, providing emotional support and words of wisdom that can help to placate your concerns, or give you the encouragement needed to know that you're not alone and that it's okay to seek out professional help. Besides providing personalized feedback, ChatGPT is also great at posing questions a therapist would ask while you're lying down on their couch (except with ChatGPT, you can be lying on your own couch). This can once again help you to work through some of your initial responses to possible mental health concerns that you may have. Then, based on your answer to the questions our therapeutic chatbot posed to you, ChatGPT can generate a list of coping and self-care strategies that can see you right, or see you through the waiting time it takes to see a professional therapist or psychiatrist.

Assist With Adding Emotion to Writing

When our mental health isn't the best, we often also become out of touch with our emotions. We struggle to express ourselves properly and our messages can be received with a very different emotional tone than we intended. Rather than giving up on sending letters, messages, and emails all together, you can make use of ChatGPT to help you generate text that captures the correct emotional response. Once again, ChatGPT is as good as the prompt you put into it for this kind of thing. If you want it to write a heartfelt apology for you, for example, make sure that you include details of who you are writing said apology for, as well as any context that would be prevalent for it to know about. Besides writing entire letters for you, ChatGPT can also help you to find the best words or phrases to express yourself fully and properly capture your feelings. If you're looking to go old-school and write your crush a love letter, but have all the words worthiness of a fifth-grader, then you can use the new-school tool of ChatGPT to help you spark those flames of passion.

Provide Emotional Intelligence Training

The final thing that makes ChatGPT a pretty neat therapist on demand is its ability to help you improve your emotional intelligence. Using its vast database, deep learning skills, and large language model, ChatGPT can think up a load of scenarios and situations for you to practice identifying the correct emotional response, or responding to situations that are emotionally charged. This can help to raise your emotional awareness, and work on ways to understand the emotions of others and to manage your own. This is particularly useful if you frequently work in high-stress situations, but aren't the most in-touch with your emotional side.

Let's Talk It Out

Now that we've covered the ways in which ChatGPT can work as your personal therapist on demand, it's time to go over some practical tips on how to engage with the chatbot as a tool for emotional support. But, before we go over the best ways to frame your questions or share feelings with the deep-learning AI, a lil' reiteration of the disclaimer given earlier: While ChatGPT is a great tool for helping you get on top of your mental health, it is in no way a substitute for a mental health-care professional. It is, however, a great first step to getting some help, providing a judgment-free ear to your problems and pains, troubles and strife, and giving some good advice to boot. As long as you word your "prompts" right, ChatGPT can be the perfect soundboard, providing you with a safe outlet to share your thoughts and express your feelings.

Engineering ChatGPT for Empathy

If you want to use ChatGPT as an assistant to your regular therapy, or are looking to use it to chat through some problems you have in your life or with your mindset, you're first going to need to learn how to engineer the chatbot for empathy.

If you've heard the term "empathy" before, but don't really know what it means, here's a definition for you. Empathy is the ability to understand and "feel" the emotions of others (Dmitriev, 2023). Unlike sympathy, which views things from your point of view as feeling sorry for the person you are sympathizing with, empathy is about walking a mile in someone else's shoes; in other words, to view things from their perspective. Empathy is made up of two parts: the affective (being able to "share" the emotional state of others) and the cognitive (being able to understand the thought processes of others and view things from their perspective) (Dmitriev, 2023).

Almost all humans are hard-wired to be empathetic in some way or form. Most of the time, we can't even help it. We see someone cut their finger or get hurt in some way, and we can't help but wince at their pain. This is because empathy is not only innate (hard-wired in us), but also instinctive (done without thinking). In many ways, it's our ability to empathize with one another that has allowed us humans to work together in larger and larger groups as we built the world around us. That being said, empathy is not a universal constant. In other words, the capacity to empathize is not the same for every person. Just like we each have different personality traits, strengths, and weaknesses, we also have different empathetic capabilities. Not only that, but we also experience different levels of empathy at different times in our lives. And it's not so clear-cut as those with money feel more empathetic, and those without less. Because as I'm sure we all know, most of the rich are not renowned for caring about anyone other than themselves, while there are many diamonds of empathy that live in some of the roughest areas the modern world has to offer.

Because of this, many emotion researchers think of empathy as an ability rather than an emotional state of being (Berkeley Edu, 2023). If it's an ability, then that means it's something that we've actively got to work on to get better at. And this is where

ChatGPT comes in as our non-judgmental, personalized empathy trainer! Let's go over the main way we can use ChatGPT to develop our empathy through replicating real-world experiences and specifically tailored scenarios.

Role-Player Pro

The first way to use ChatGPT for training your empathic abilities is to have it role-play different "characters" whose perspective you want to practice seeing things from. Also known as perspective-taking, this involves trying to imagine yourself "in someone else's shoes," seeing a specific scenario from their point of view. Perspective-taking is considered to be the best way to develop empathy in adults (Dmitriev, 2023). As we saw with our "act as" prompts from Chapter 3, ChatGPT is able to take on personas as easily as you can engineer the prompt telling it to do so. Simulation is the name of the AI game, and ChatGPT is no different.

If you want to use ChatGPT in a role-play kind of exercise to work on your empathy, begin by selecting the type of person or social group that you want to practice empathizing with. Then, engineer your prompt based on this person or group. Such a prompt could go something like: "Let's role-play. You will be an X type of person from a Y social background. Introduce yourself and then wait to answer my questions."

After ChatGPT has introduced itself as the character it is role-playing, then comes the time to ask it questions. These can be related to the simulated character's hopes, fears, wants, or needs. They can be about their daily life or even about their dreams. Remember that the longer the conversation goes on, the more accurate ChatGPT becomes, which means that the more you chat with this simulated character, the more life-like their responses will become.

Prompts to Use for Your Therapist on Demand

In this final section, we're going to go over a list of prompts for using ChatGPT as your therapist on demand. Remember that ChatGPT fills more of a "therapist-assistant" role rather than filling the role of a fully-fledged mental health professional, and doesn't compete when compared to seeking actual help and advice. But, as a first-step or as a supplement to your usual therapy sessions, ChatGPT can be a great aid. And, as we've seen, it's also an excellent way to practice getting in touch with your emotions, improve your emotional intelligence, and practice your empathic skills. With that out of the way, let's get on with it!

- "Act as a therapist having a conversation with a [enter info about yourself] seeking to share their thoughts and feelings about [insert challenge here]. Read the situation and ask questions aimed at helping me improve my understanding, and prepare a list of self-help tips and guidance on how to deal with this challenge."
- "Act as a psychologist providing mental support to [enter info about yourself]. Use therapeutic and psychological counseling techniques, such as active listening and non-judgmental questioning, to provide empathetic responses aimed at helping me manage my emotions. Here is my first question…"

- "Act as a mental health advisor giving advice on how to manage the stresses and mental fatigue associated with X profession. Make use of theories from mental health care, as well as meditation and mindfulness practices. My first request is…"
- "You are Dr. X, a kind and approachable therapist renowned for your emotional intelligence. Pose thoughtful questions and provide insightful and actionable advice on how to deal with Y. Use a friendly, conversational tone rather than listing points."
- "Act as a life coach with 10 years of expertise in your field. I will provide you with details about a certain life goal and challenges I am facing achieving it. Generate suggestions on how to overcome these challenges using simple and empathic language, as well as come up with an actionable plan for overcoming these challenges and achieving my goal."

With the end of chapter four, we now know how to use ChatGPT to not only assist us in our personal and professional lives, but also how to provide us with emotional assistance and mental health advice. But wait, there's more! Because our multi-skilled, deep learning chatbot can also be a revolutionary tool in the world of business. Now that we've seen how ChatGPT can be a comforting and assistive presence in your personal life, let's have a look at how its skill set can be used to enhance your professional life, too. Turn on over to chapter five as we learn how ChatGPT can become your ultimate business partner, right in your pocket!

Chapter 5
Your Pocket-sized Business Partner

Welcome, my soon to be ChatGPT-savvy reader, to chapter five! As we saw in the previous chapter, ChatGPT can take on many different personas, professional or otherwise. It can even take on the role of a therapist on demand to provide personalized support and assistance for your mental health. Now, it's time to move on from the personal way that our chatbot can assist you to the professional, as we learn how ChatGPT can serve as your personalized, pocket-sized business partner.

As we shall come to see, ChatGPT can help to redefine your business communication, revolutionize your marketing content, and even provide in-depth analytics to aid in the decision-making process for your company. It's the impactful analyst, the unsleeping customer rep, the guru digital marketer, the one, the only... ChatGPT! Let's go over how it can save (and even make) you money.

Redefining Business Communication

Communication is one of the cornerstones of the business world. We communicate with loads of different people on a daily basis, whether it be with our team, suppliers, or most importantly, with our customers and clients. Communication is involved in every aspect of business and is a key skill for every entrepreneur to master. But you can't just talk at people and expect to get results; you need to learn how to communicate effectively.

The Importance of Effective Communication

Effective communication results in both sides (the imparter and receiver of the information) leaving a conversation confident that they are on the same page, and have the same understanding of what the conversation was about and what is expected of them going forward. To use ChatGPT terminology, effective communication is about engineering the prompts you use in order to generate the best (and most accurate) results possible, without any misunderstandings getting in the way. This is a lot harder to achieve than people think, especially when other people are involved in the decision-making process. If you want to become successful in business, you need to learn how to communicate effectively. Luckily, you're not on your own when it comes to learning the ins and outs of how to communicate effectively. Once again, ChatGPT has your back as the perfect business assistant; ready and waiting to teach you all about effective communication tips, tricks, and techniques, to make you a personalized strategy and action plan that you can implement into your business model, and even take over a lot of the business communication "grunt work." But more on that in the next section. For now, we're going to go over why effective communication is so important for business and how it can make you better at business too.

Builds Strong Relationships

The first thing that effective communication helps us with is building strong relationships. Whether it be with employees, clients, suppliers, or customers, strong relationships are essential. From the outset, it can seem tricky to sow the seeds of a healthy, strong relationship with someone, but it's actually quite simple: Begin with good conversations. We can think of conversations, along with experiences, as the building blocks of relationships. The more good conversations we have with someone, the more we enjoy their company, and the more we want to have them around or to help them out.

We all know that person who has the "gift of the gab," who seems able to speak easily and confidently about any and all topics, and who wins people over with the sheer prowess of their conversation skills. This is what a business owner or entrepreneur needs to master if they are to succeed in building strong relationships. Internal relationships between you and your team are a make-or-break factor for your business and often determine the company culture, as well as its overall productivity levels. External relationships with your clients, customers, and suppliers are essential to growing your business successfully, increasing customer retention, and creating a positive and inviting image of your company. The more pleasant someone's experience with your business is, the more likely they are to come back again in the future. This requires creating personal bonds and personalized messages with, and for, your business connections.

Employee Management

If you are in a role where you have to manage other humans, then you definitely need to be an effective communicator. The more skilled a manager is at communicating, the more likely it is that their team will understand what is expected of them, how to complete their tasks, and how long they have to complete them. More than that though, a successful manager will also provide clear and positively worded feedback, improving the effectiveness of their team, and of course, giving praise for achievements. This is the way to manage humans effectively, and it all comes from effective communication.

Decision Making Aid

Besides helping to build stronger relationships and better manage your team, effective communication is also a key enhancer of a company's decision-making process. The quicker you can communicate your points effectively, the quicker a decision can be made. This, in turn, makes your company more agile, giving it the competitive edge over businesses that can't communicate as effectively, and as such, are chained down by a long process of decision-making back and forth. If you can outline all the pros and cons of the various options in simple terms where misunderstanding is minimized, then there will be less questions and less uncertainty. There will also be more of a feeling coming from your shareholders, staff members, or customers that you know what you're doing and can be trusted to lead the company forth to greener pastures, making everyone richer as you do so.

Innovation Stimulator

With effective communication within a business comes the growth of a company culture that symbolizes openness, collaboration, and camaraderie. These all result in enhancing creativity and innovation at every level of the organization, increasing the overall success of your business brand. How do you begin doing this? Make the individuals that are your employees feel like their voice is heard and their opinions are valued through communicating with them effectively.

Business Grower and Brand Developer

The overall result of being an effective communicator is that your business will be more successful than those run by owners who don't feel the need to communicate effectively. All areas of your business, whether internal or external, are improved by an effective communication system. Everything, from your relationship with the bank to your business brand, is enhanced by the leader understanding how to communicate effectively. Since the birth of social media introduced the need for every business to have an online presence, it is essential for customer loyalty and retention to build a strong and personable brand. Once again, effective communication is the key to this.

But enough speaking up the importance of this business skill, let's turn to looking at how ChatGPT can turn you into a master communicator capable of inspiring peak performance in every aspect of your business.

ChatGPT: The Business Communication Specialist

As we mentioned in chapter one, the acronym GPT stands for generative pre-trained transformer. This means that our chatbot can not only understand the context of the conversation (based on other messages in the thread), but can also generate appropriate and (if your prompt is engineered correctly) accurate responses based on your current question and the context that has been created for it so far. In other words, ChatGPT is quite the communication specialist and can be put to great use throughout every sphere of your business, from customer relations to internal memos and supplier communications. Effective communication is essential for the successful running of an organization, and as we shall see, ChatGPT is your perfect tool to finesse this key business area. Let's go over the main ways you can start using ChatGPT to improve the effectiveness of your business communications.

Customer Service and Support

As we've chatted about a few times already, one thing that ChatGPT really excels at is customer service. The LLM's ability to accurately understand customer queries and provide them with complete answers and actionable solutions makes it invaluable to every business that deals directly with its customers or clients. Add to this the fact that it's active 24/7 and can talk to a large number of customers at the same time, and you've got the golden goose of customer service response systems. Using ChatGPT to help out with your customer queries not only improves the effectiveness of your business communication, but has also been seen to increase customer satisfaction. Yup, you read that right, people can actually find ChatGPT easier to deal with than human customer service agents (Dermitzakis, 2023).

Internal Communication

Besides helping take care of your customer queries, ChatGPT is also an excellent tool for streamlining your internal business communications. When it comes to sending out reminders, updates, or memos, there's nothing better than delegating as much as you can to AI. Keep all your team members up to date with the great communication automator that is ChatGPT. Whether it be taking care of routine communications, or assisting with scheduling and sending out invites for meetings, ChatGPT has you covered, ready to enhance the efficiency of your organization through improving the effectiveness of your internal communications.

Content Generation

ChatGPT can also serve as your business communication specialist by creating content quicker than it takes you to engineer the prompt telling it what content creation task it needs to complete. So far we've seen how ChatGPT can help you to create content for social media and websites, but it can also create other forms of written content too, such as emails and reports, presentations and pitches. Remember though, just like you would read through and edit the content created by one of your employees or freelancers, so too will you have to do the same with ChatGPT. An added bonus of our AI business communication specialist, is that it can produce content in a wide variety of styles using the perfect tone for the audience that will read it. All that you need is to include these details in the prompt you engineer for the task.

Multilingual Support

If your company is spread over different parts of the world, or has a multinational staff or audience, then ChatGPT could be the multilingual support tool you've been waiting for. OpenAI's awesome creation can understand and generate content in over 50 languages, and that number is just set to grow in the future. With the international, multinational, and multicultural nature of the internet, it is fast becoming an essential skill for any business website chatbot to be able to detect the language entered by a potential customer, to understand their query, and to generate a reply in the same language. This can spell the difference between a frustrated customer who feels your company doesn't care about them, and a pleasantly surprised customer who had their query answered, felt listened to, and understood. I'm sure we all know which one is more likely to buy something from you in the future.

Data Analysis

ChatGPT can further help you to perfect your effective communication skills by performing detailed data analysis for you. Not only can it access and analyze the data you need in the time it takes a human to power up their laptop, but it can also display said data in easy-to-understand reports, highlighting key insights and even making recommendations to help with the decision-making process. Besides analyzing data, ChatGPT can also help you with data entry, helping to reduce errors and improve the accuracy and efficiency of all data-related tasks.

Market Research

Linked to data analysis is ChatGPT's ability to help you with that all important business task of conducting market research. The powerful think tank can help you to identify market trends, understand customer wants and needs, and gather key insights that will not only make you a more effective communicator, but will also give you that all important edge over your competition. To help you gain the upper hand over your competition, ChatGPT can gather any and all public information about them, using this to create a competitor analysis that highlights the strengths and weaknesses of their business model. You can also ask ChatGPT to compare and contrast your business with your competitors, checking how you match up with their product lines, prices, profits, and so on. This can help you to effectively communicate to potential investors why they should invest in your company, and not one of your competitors.

Besides helping you to better understand your competition, our business communication specialist can also provide key insights as to the demographics of your target market. It does this by analyzing consumer trends, collecting and collating data on how best to approach different demographic groups, and developing buyer personas (detailed descriptions of your ideal customers or target audience).

Finally, ChatGPT can enhance your market research by collecting and organizing customer feedback. Almost as essential as making a sale is getting feedback on your product or service. Without knowing what people think about your product or service, you won't know what works and what needs to be worked on. ChatGPT can take the feedback given from customer queries on your website, feedback given on apps, or from your email campaign (run by ChatGPT too, I'd hope), analyze it, and organize it according to type and category. It can also draw key trends from this dataset and even put it in neat lil' graphs for you, making it as easy to understand, and as easy to communicate as possible.

The Wordsmith

In the age of Instagram influencers and TikTok celebrities, everyone who's anyone needs to have a presence online, and needs to look damn good while doing so. A business is no exception. It's almost like it happened overnight; all of a sudden, businesses had to have their own social presence and become active on social media platforms. This puts a lot of pressure on a company, especially considering how judgmental the internet can be of a business putting out sub-par content. As such, every business owner needs to make sure that their organization is bringing their A game when it comes to the content they're releasing onto the socials.

As we've touched on a few times so far, one of the major perks (and major advancements) of ChatGPT is its ability to generate content. While the content generated might not be up to the standards of a professional human writer, it's a whole lot better, more researched, and more detailed, than the average Joe could produce. Besides, even those pro writers need someone else to go over and edit their work for them. As such, we can think of ChatGPT as being far more of a wordsmith than the general public, and can produce some pretty fantastic content for your business. Plus, ChatGPT generates detailed content in a matter of seconds, so spending a lil' time doing human editing afterwards still saves you time in the long run! When running your own company, time becomes the second major currency in your life, and if you can save some of it through using ChatGPT to help you create high-quality content, then I say go for it!

The Importance of High-Quality Content

When it comes to turning a potential sale into a returning customer, there are few things that work better than communicating effectively with your audience through content marketing. Sure, you need to have a good product or service first, but after that is secured, the next step is to start telling people about it and trying to get them interested enough to buy it. As great as your product may be, if no one knows about it, nobody's going to buy it.

Depending on the size of your business, you should be spending between 5 to 25% of your revenue on marketing, and of that, around 30% should be spent on the creation and dissemination of high-quality content (Riserbato, 2021). But this cost is nothing when compared to what you get out of it when done right. According to many marketing experts, creating high-quality, engaging content, and doing so consistently, has the greatest impact on the decision-making process of potential customers (Riserbato, 2021). Let's go over some of the main benefits of quality content marketing, before in the next section, showing how ChatGPT can create this primetime content for you.

Develop a Following

Just like those Instagram or TikTok influencers, your business can also benefit from developing a following on various social media platforms. Having high-quality content will ensure that your customers enjoy seeing your posts pop up in their feed. The positive experience they have engaging with your killer content also makes them hang around on your page or website, as well as far more likely to come back again. Through this, you'll develop a deeper bond with your audience as they trust in the story you tell through your content.

Customers don't buy things just for the trust they have in the product, but also because of the trust they have in the business that makes it. The trick to creating a following is to build rapport through consistently creating value without expecting anything in return. Through doing so, you'll increase the trust people have in your brand, improve the reputation of your business, and overall, enhance the positive association people have with your products and services. If that isn't a winning way to create a rock-solid customer base, I don't know what is.

Heighten Your Brand Visibility Through SEO

As we mentioned above, one of the great things about having quality content is that it builds rapport and trust with your target audience. This is done through consistently producing content that appears in people's feeds or shows up when they search for a related term on Google or on the socials. But how do you get your content to show up on their feeds and in their searches in the first place? For that, you need to heighten your brand visibility through optimizing your content for search engines. This is known as search engine optimization, or SEO, and is one of the essential ingredients to gaining traction from your content marketing efforts. Basically, what good SEO does is identify the most searched or searchable words and phrases that your target audience uses, and then includes them in the content being produced. This means that, when your target audience searches for something using these keywords, your content will pop up under the suggested search results. The better the SEO, the higher up the search results your content will go. High-quality business content takes SEO in its stride and heightens the entire brand's visibility through doing so.

Become an Authority in Your Industry

By creating a trustworthy and reliable brand that disseminates high-quality (SEO approved) content on the regular, you'll soon position your company as an "influencer." This will build credibility, both among your target audience and with your competitors, making your business an expert or authority in your industry. All achieved through creating consistently high-quality and engaging content. If you're considered a pro in your field, more people are likely to trust that you know what's going on and that you know what's good for them (i.e., buying what your business is selling). It will also mean that people are more likely to recommend your product or service to others rather than that of your competitors. People will even start recommending your product without ever having used it themselves, all based on the brand image you've portrayed in your high-quality marketing!

Save Money

Although it may cost you more time, effort, and money when producing it, high-quality content will not just save, but make you more money in the long run. According to HubSpot, a giant in the software product marketing field, content marketing has "remained the most cost-effective marketing strategy available" (Riserbato, 2021). This was true when they first started analyzing the field of content marketing 10 years ago, and remains so today.

While the upfront costs of producing high-quality content have historically been pretty steep, this is no longer the case now that the new content marketing game-changing player ChatGPT has entered the fray. But even back when quality content marketing carried a hefty start-up cost, it still paid itself off and then some when viewed over the long term. Imagine how much more that can grow with ChatGPT cutting those upfront costs down to size.

ChatGPT as Your Content Creation Guru

As we've seen so far, the sky is pretty much the limit when it comes to the various uses of ChatGPT. Or, to put it more accurately, the prompt's the limit. If you engineer your prompt just right, ChatGPT won't just half the time it takes to produce high-quality content, it will fractionalize it. According to Julia McCoy from Content At Scale, what in the past took content marketers four hours to produce can be generated by ChatGPT in under five minutes (McCoy, 2023).

There are loads of different kinds of content you can produce with ChatGPT, including posts and captions for social media, emails and newsletters, descriptions for your products, outlines for blogs, and even copy for your website's landing page. As we said above, the prompt's the limit. Through incorporating this powerful content creation tool into your marketing plan, you'll cut costs, save time, and be assured of consistent quality content that is delivered on schedule, and that is tailored to resonate with your specific target audience. Let's go over the numerous ways in which ChatGPT can be used as your wordsworthy content creation guru.

Research and Development

With the power of its 570 gigs database, ChatGPT knows more than any human ever could, and has a better memory recall than all of us. Besides this massive aid to the world of research, ChatGPT has another benefit when it comes to research and development. As we covered in the previous chapter, ChatGPT has the impressive skill of being able to impersonate people from a variety of different backgrounds, both professional and personal. This means that you can prompt it to take on the perspective of your target audience, let's say, and ask it to give you feedback on how engaging it finds the content or the content ideas you've got from this point of view.

Besides asking it to take the viewpoint of your ideal customer, you can also prompt ChatGPT to take on a wide variety of personas or perspectives for people that might engage with your content. For example, you could tell ChatGPT to take on the perspective of someone who buys your customer's products, or that is of a different demographic to your current customer base, to see what they would think about (and how they'd engage with) your content. Finally, you could engineer prompts focused on the different social media platforms or online channels and see how ChatGPT would interact with your content from these different perspectives. It can also provide feedback on how to tailor your content for these various marketing channels and help you develop a plan to personalize your content for the audiences of these different platforms.

Planning and Preparing Content Outlines

Along with research and development, ChatGPT can also assist with many other steps in the planning stages of your content marketing plan. You could ask it to give you a list of topics your target audience would find interesting or would engage with. Then, you can ask it to brainstorm possible blog posts, social media posts, or newsletter articles based on these topics. And we're not done yet! After that, you can prompt ChatGPT to produce an outline for a blog, etc. tailored to your target audience. Remember to enter your different topics individually for the highest quality results. Also, remember that the longer the thread, the more accurate and personalized ChatGPT's results become, so keep it all in the same thread.

Crib Notes and Summaries

One thing about thinking up interesting, researched, and industry-specific content is that you need to read a lot of interesting research specific to your industry in turn. Once more, ChatGPT has your back for this. You can ask it to find the best blogs, books, or articles to read based on the list of topics it generated for you. You can then ask it to summarize (one at a time) this content, providing bullet point notes or abstract-style summaries to once again save you that most precious of resources: time. Furthermore, you can ask ChatGPT to focus on certain aspects of the content, prompting it to only summarize information related to those aspects.

You can get creative with this, even asking ChatGPT to summarize fiction books for you, or to provide a synopsis of a TV show so that you can decide whether or not it's worth a watch. This, once again, shows how ChatGPT can save you some time. And, little by little, all these snips of time that our deep learning chatbot saves you add up to you having a lot more of this resource to play with.

Content Drafting

While ChatGPT isn't necessarily going to produce engagement-primed, high-quality content first time 'round when asking it to write a blog post for you, neither would a human. As renowned author Sir Terry Pratchett once said, "The first draft is just you telling yourself the story" (in Fox, 2019). If you substitute "you" for "ChatGPT," then you get the picture of what I'm trying to say. It's not that ChatGPT can't produce some pretty great content at times, just that we shouldn't expect it to get it right on the first draft.

ChatGPT can also take on the role of an editor or writing coach, "coaching" you through the writing of your content. It can provide information on the best ways to write a beginning or ending paragraph for a persuasive blog post, give you in-time feedback of what your target audience would think of a certain phrase, provide lists of the best SEO words and phrases to use based on your topic, and provide editorial feedback and suggestions on how to polish and shine your draft into some darn fine high-quality content.

Crafting Proposals

Last but not least, ChatGPT can help to craft proposals of a wide variety of types and for any topic you can think of. You could, for example, ask ChatGPT to generate a proposal for a short pottery course, or you could prompt it to draft a business proposal tailored toward a specific investor. Product proposals, grant proposals, investment proposals, and more, ChatGPT has examples of each and all in its dataset, and as such, can generate it up for you. How tailored and audience-specific the proposal is depends, once again, on the prowess of your prompt. But if your prompt game is strong, then boy can ChatGPT help to present your business as a professional organization that has its

A game on display in its content, and the assumption will go in every other aspect of the business too.

The Silent Analyst

Besides business communication and quality content creation, the third way that ChatGPT can serve as your pocket-sized business partner is by providing you with those all-important business data analytics. One of the cornerstones of business success is having information on what's working and what's not, what your customers want, and where your competitors are succeeding or struggling. This info comes in the form of data known as analytics.

According to Investopedia, data analytics is "the science of analyzing raw data to make conclusions about that information" (Frankenfield (2023). Through analyzing said data, businesses become more capable of meeting their customer's wants and needs. Data analytics also serve to optimize the internal processes of a business, allowing it to perform at higher levels of efficiency, make more informed and strategic decisions, and through all of these, reach those lofty peaks of increased profitability. There are many different ways to analyze the data, just as there are loads of different datasets to collect, collate, investigate, and interpret. Some of the main approaches to data analytics include:

- Descriptive analytics (describing or determining what happened).

- Diagnostic analytics (detailing why something happened).
- Predictive analytics (predicting what's going to happen).
- Prescriptive analytics (stipulating what should be done next).

The Benefits of Prioritizing Data Analytics

As you can see from the main types of data analytics listed above, there are a mass amount of different datasets to be analyzed. These can reach from historical data to that of the present situation, and even reach through to the future through trying to predict or prescribe the best course of action going forward. Without such analytics, it would be left up to the winds of fate and the ever-changing whims of customers whether or not a business succeeds or fails. Since that would be a pretty bad business model, it behooves every entrepreneur or boss to develop an in-depth understanding of the data analytics related to their business.

In this section, we're going to outline the best benefits staying on top of your data analytics has for your business before, in the next, detailing how ChatGPT, the data analyst supreme, can keep you and your company getting better and better (aka richer and richer) through doing a lot of the data analyzing grunt work for you.

Insight Generator

Have you heard the term "digital footprint" before? It refers to the trail of data you leave in your tracks as you traverse through the digital world, aka. the internet. While this is generally viewed as a bad thing for the average person (as it often includes personal searches or information we'd rather wasn't linked to us or wasn't readily available for marketers to use), it is invaluable to businesses. Analyzing the data from your customer's digital footprints can provide key insights that provide a window into the world of your target audience's likes and dislikes, what they are interested in, and what else they are spending their money on. Through collecting a large amount of this data, you'll also be able to identify behavioral trends and spending patterns for your target market, allowing you to customize your products to reflect these trends and patterns. Analyzing your customer's digital footprint also means that you get to know them a lot better, personalizing them for you, and in turn, showing you how you make your business seem personable for them. The more you understand your target audience, the better you'll be able to picture who they are and what they want. The better you know this, the more you can customize your content and marketing accordingly. The end result: A more trusting, loyal customer base that feels like you are "one of them."

Decision-Making Aid

As we've mentioned before, decision-making is part and parcel of being a business owner. And boy can some of those decisions be tough to make. The better informed you are about all aspects of each option, the more likely you are to make the right choice when the time comes. While it may be nigh impossible to predict every outcome of a decision that you have to make, every little bit counts. In other words, the more data you have to analyze, the better. Although taking more time at the get-go, data analytics can save you time, money, and a whole lot of energy. There's nothing worse than being two months down the line on a project or new marketing strategy, only to realize that a totally avoidable oversight in the decision-making process is going to drag you back to step one.

Businesses that incorporate data analytics in their decision-making processes also set their organizations up for proactivity. In other words, if you incorporate a load of data analytics and data analyzing processes in your business model, you allow your team to easily identify potential opportunities and for you to easily validate the potential of these opportunities too.

Marketing Campaign Insights

It can be tough for a business to work out their various marketing campaigns and all of the content required within each of them. For businesses that don't use data analytics, that is. Those that do analyze data from their target audience (which, let's be honest, should be everyone) are easily able to identify what type of content their audience is after, and as such, can better tailor their marketing campaigns for their clientele. Through analyzing trends in customer purchasing habits and monitoring online web traffic and conversion rates, you'll be able to, with some degree of accuracy, figure out what's working and what's not, and predict what the next best move is for your marketing efforts.

Through acting on the market trends you pick up from your data analytics, you'll be able to take advantage of the changes to customer behavior that would otherwise have blindsided a less informed business. While you go from strength to analytics savvy strength, the blindsided business has had to close their doors, allowing you to further expand your market share and attract their customer base through your targeted marketing campaigns. All thanks to them data analytics.

Fix Problems and Minimize Risks

Besides insights, decision-making, and marketing campaigns, another massive benefit of data analytics is that it can help you to iron out the kinks in your business model or organizational operations. Through analyzing the data you collect about your business, you can highlight operational inefficiencies and begin working out a game plan for how to refine and streamline them. By collecting and collating data from customer feedback, and comparing it to data from the manufacturing process of what you sell, you can figure out ways to optimize your product or service for the customers while still remaining within the realms of profitability.

As your business grows in size, there will also be the need to streamline your various business operations in order to reduce costs and further maximize those sweet profits. Not only can data analytics highlight opportunities to improve your business, but it can also help to mitigate risks. By analyzing the trends and key findings of your business and marketing data, you become more aware of the inner workings of your organization. This means you'll be better placed to find and deal with potential risks to your business than someone who doesn't analyze that data.

Identify Opportunities and Drive Innovation

The final way that data analytics can improve your business is through helping you to identify potential opportunities for it. One of the keys to remaining in the business game for as long as you can is to keep on the cutting edge of innovation. As we've seen so far, through analyzing data you'll generate insights, develop a deeper understanding of your target audience, be able to make more informed decisions, identify any problems that may arise with your business operations, and even mitigate many of the avoidable risks that plague any pursuit of making money. This all serves to support and drive that all-important business grower: innovation. According to McKinsey & Company, one of the "big three" strategy consulting firms in the world, innovation is "the ability to conceive, develop, deliver, and scale new products, services, processes, and business models for customers" (McKinsey & Company, 2022).

Besides developing new products and services, or improving your current ones, innovation also includes any change or development to your business that increases its value or serves to further drive growth in some way. Whether innovation comes in the form of a new PR strategy or an updated product range, it all stems from the same place: data analytics. In order to identify opportunities, you need to know what they are. In order to make the most of these opportunities, you need to know what you are and how you can use this to successfully seize hold of the opportunity, and innovate your way to greener and more profitable pastures.

Data Analytics Made Easy With ChatGPT

Now that we've made clear just how important data analytics are for you and your business, let's learn how to make your data analyzing life easy through using our friendly Jack-of-many-trades deep learning LLM, ChatGPT. As you might expect, out of the multitude of uses and tools that ChatGPT possesses, analyzing data can be considered its bread and butter. There are many ways that our handy lil' chatbot can help out with collecting, collating, and analyzing data, even going as far as to highlight key trends or potential opportunities to grow and improve for you!

Since its creation in 2022, ChatGPT has rapidly become an invaluable tool for data analysis. No matter how large or small your business may be at present, ChatGPT can help you grow it through streamlining your data analytics, improving the communicability of your data, and even taking over a lot of the data analyzing work for you! Let's go over the main ways that you can start using ChatGPT to enhance your business analytics today.

Making Data Understandable

The first obvious use of ChatGPT in data analytics is to analyze the data for you. But what OpenAI's creation can do that no previous digital data analyst could do, is to interpret this data and write it out in plain English, telling the "story" of the dataset and making it accessible to the average person. Our AI data analyzer can scan through your customer feedback, for example, and highlight key trends, opportunities, or risks that your company faces based on said data. Not only that, but it can put all of these key highlights together in a well-written, perfectly structured report that makes this data understandable for us humans. You could use ChatGPT to analyze your financial data, as another example. It can then use this data to generate financial performance analyses or even create a budgeting plan for you based on your spending habits. Whatever dataset you decide to analyze, ChatGPT can also interpret it and make it understandable for us non-data analysts.

Automate the Process of Data Analysis

One of the best things about ChatGPT, or computational devices and algorithms in general, is that they can work out in seconds what takes us humans hours to complete. Whether it's a mathematical equation to solve, a dataset to organize and analyze, or some complicated programming code to write, AI has us humans beat in the speed, and increasingly, the accuracy of the output. ChatGPT's ability to instantaneously organize a certain data set and to write reports highlighting key trends in a matter of seconds, means that you can automate a lot of processes related to data analysis, freeing up more of that most valuable resource: time. It can also be incredibly useful during meetings or brainstorming sessions. Providing real-time results, rather than having to wait for the next meeting to discuss things further, also benefits the innovation and decision-making processes too. The automation of data analytics brought about by ChatGPT allows you to keep growing, improving, and responding to market changes faster than your competition can. Data analytics and ChatGPT: A winning combo for business success if ever there was one.

Interview and Meeting Prep

If you're looking for the perfect tool to help you prepare for that job interview or important meeting, look no further than ChatGPT. If you don't think that either of these has anything to do with data analytics, let me show you the error of your ways. If you want to ace that job interview, you should develop an understanding for what that business is about and how it is doing. To find out what a business is about, you look at their website. To find out how a business is doing, you look at the data. Similarly, with an important meeting, you need to understand the position of all people in the meeting. In other words, you need to analyze their available data and balance it out compared to the other meeting attendees. For a human, doing this kind of preparation could take hours, even days. For our deep-learning AI, it takes a matter of minutes, and most of those are spent writing, rewriting, and tweaking your prompts.

Another thing that ChatGPT can assist with in terms of interview and meeting prep is to take on the role of the person that will be interviewing you or attending the meeting. You can ask ChatGPT to ask you questions about you, or your presentation, from different perspectives or viewpoints, ask it for constructive feedback on your presentation, or even have it co-write your speaking points!

Takes Care of the Coding Side of Things

If you're like me, then coding is a language, or group of languages, that you just never learned to speak. But never fear! ChatGPT is here to take care of that for you. As we mentioned earlier in the book, the "hottest new programming language" is the English language. As such, if you're like me, we're now in good stead to become coding pros! Or to seem like one at least, with the help of ChatGPT. In the past, whenever coding became involved in data analytics, the not-so-tech-savvy entrepreneur or business owner would either have to hire someone that could do the coding side, outsource it to a freelancer, or just give up. Now, you can delegate the task to ChatGPT and have that illegible code written up in no time at all, and have it produced by AI for (in some ways) AI. Not only can ChatGPT generate code for you, but it can also optimize it too. Code optimization means making long code shorter and easier to understand. With ChatGPT as the translator, coding has become accessible for everyone.

The Unsleeping Customer Rep

I'm sure you've heard the saying "the customer is always right" before. While we may want to disagree with this old adage at times, one thing is true: If we don't treat our customers right, they're going to take their hard-earned dollars elsewhere. How do you stop this from happening? Through having great customer service, of course!

The Benefits of Great Customer Service

Establishing killer customer service involves listening to your target audience and showing that you value your customers' opinions. Your company culture and your customer service go hand-in-hand to create your brand image. With customers now able to contact businesses directly through their websites, or to air their complaints to their followers on social media pages, tagging your poor business in the process, developing and keeping a positive brand image is more important than ever before. And it all starts with great customer service. Let's go through the main benefits good customer service has for your business, before helping you rest at ease by knowing you can have the large majority of customer service tasks covered by our unsleeping customer rep, ChatGPT.

Build Customer Loyalty

Developing a strong and steadfast customer base is (or should be) the aim of each and every business out there. If you don't have customers, you're not going to make sales. If you don't sell your product or service, then you don't have a business, you have a very expensive hobby. But just selling what you've got going on to a one-and-done customer is not enough in the modern world. You're going to need to keep selling, and keep on keeping on selling, for as long as your business doors stay open. You could keep trying to attract new customers, ever increasing your customer base, but this isn't a very effective way of doing business. It's much better (and more profitable) to retain your customers, encouraging customer loyalty, through fostering a strong brand image and a reputation for quality in every aspect of your company. This begins, first of all, by having a quality product, and secondly, through having quality customer service.

Retaining your current customers and enticing them to make repeat purchases has been proven, time and again, to be more cost-effective and more profitable than trying to constantly get new ones (Mailchimp, 2023). By providing a personalized, unique purchasing experience, and making interacting with your business as pleasant as possible, people will enjoy what you've got going on, making them more likely to come back for more. Soon, people will actually *want* to be customers of your business, as you've made them feel like they're a part of your success, and best of all, they'll *want* to help you succeed.

According to a study carried out by Salesforce titled *State of the Connected Customer*, a whopping 89% of online customers were found to be more willing or likely to make another purchase if they had a pleasant experience with the site they were buying from (Afshar, 2023). As with the online world, so with the physical one. Think of it like a first date. If you are strictly business and want to get down to the deal ASAP, then you might get some one-and-done action, but chances are you're not going to get a second date. However, if you make that first date a memorable experience, you'll be more likely to seal the deal on the regular. Even if you don't make the sale the first time, chances are that there will be a second, third, or even fourth interaction after that where you do. The bottom line: The better your customer service skills, the more likely customers are to come back for more.

Through being consistent with your great customer service, you'll build up a loyal customer base committed to you and your brand, who will keep selecting your services over your competition's time and again. But remember to keep things fresh and interesting through offering rewards programs, providing discounts, and making sure your customer service is more than just talk.

Develop a Strong Company Culture

If you have great customer service, chances are that the rest of your company culture is pretty spot-on too. This is because by prioritizing your customer service, you are thinking about business the right way. Nothing in a business is isolated; every nook and cranny forms a part of the body known as an organization.

As such, every part influences the other, either for better or for worse. A company's culture can be thought of as the "personality" of the business, including its quirks, beliefs, attitudes, and even psychological state. It can also be thought of as the story of your company and how people—both customers and employees—view and engage with it. Through telling a good company story, and following it through with actions to back up the words, you'll develop a brand of repute.

When developing your company culture, begin by defining what exactly it is. What is the "personality" of your organization? What core values do you want it to represent? How is your company unique (i.e., different from the competition)? What customers are you servicing and how can you serve them best?

Referrals and Voluntary Brand Ambassadors

When we run into a problem we can't solve ourselves, or something that we own breaks, we often phone up someone (aka mom or dad) that we think could know the perfect person to help us. In other words, we seek out a referral. This isn't only reserved to fixing things either. We often ask people if they know someone who can do X, is selling Y, or might be able to help us out with Z. If they do, said person proudly lets us know that they've got a prime recommendation for us. We get our recommendation, our friend or family member feels good for helping us out, and the referred-to person or company gets more business. Everyone benefits in some way and is that little bit happier, and in the case of the referred-to business, a little bit wealthier too.

This is known as word-of-mouth marketing and is the oldest, cheapest, and most effective way to increase your target market. To become the referred-to business, all you need to have is a quality product and great customer service. Referrals are a powerful way to drive sales through getting your customers to do the marketing leg-work for you! In this way, your customers become brand ambassadors, spreading the good word about your business far and wide, and throughout their social circles. But bear in mind that as helpful as a good referral is, a bad referral (i.e., someone speaking negatively about your business) does just as much harm, if not more.

Improves the Happiness of Your Team

Through making taking care of your customers right a priority of your business, you'll develop a positive and happy work environment. If you care for your customers and build strong relationships with them, chances are that your team members will too. This can make the workplace feel more like a caring community than a commercially driven organization. As the peeps at Mailchimp say: "Happier customers tend to lead to happier employees" (Mailchimp, 2023). If you foster positive and professional relationships with your customer base or target audience, that's the energy your team will reflect. If your customer service plan can be summed up as "damage control," then you'll end up with frustrated, irate customers and burnt-out, stressed, and generally unhappy employees. To stop this scenario from taking place, replace your damage control policy with a more proactive, productive, and profitable customer service strategy of building strong relationships between your team and your customers.

ChatGPT as Your Customer Service Rep

One of the foremost industries to adopt chatbots and incorporate advancements in LLMs into their business operations is the customer service industry. Marketing has always been on the frontier of the latest advancements in AI and technology in general. According to a study carried out by McKinsey Research Group, 90% of business owners, entrepreneurs, and commercial leaders are working on plans to incorporate generative AI into a variety of different parts of their businesses within the next two years (Dilmegani, 2023). While 90% may want, or plan, to incorporate AI throughout their organization, only 50% actually know what deep learning LLMs like ChatGPT are really about, and how to use them to get that competitive edge. Having made it this far into the book, you can definitely now count yourself among the 50% that knows what's going on. In this section, we'll give you even more of a tech-based head-start over your competition by outlining the various ways you can begin using ChatGPT to improve your customer service today. But first, why exactly is ChatGPT a useful tool for customer service?

Well, first of all, as the title to this overall section said, ChatGPT is the unsleeping customer rep, available 24/7, 365. This means that customers can get immediate responses to their questions and queries. Not only that, but these responses are becoming more and more "humanesque" and less mechanical or automated, all thanks to ChatGPT and generative AI. ChatGPT is also more consistent in its responses than us emotionally driven humans are. Chatbots answer each and every question or query with the same level of polite professionalism, no matter how many times that day they've been asked that question, or how dumb it may be. Furthermore, ChatGPT has no life outside of work. This means that it won't take its bad breakup out on the poor customer that just happens to ask the "wrong question," for example. Finally, it saves you time and money to use ChatGPT as your first-contact customer service rep. If that's not reason enough to begin using it, I don't know what is. Let's now go through the main ways to use ChatGPT as your unsleeping customer service representative supreme.

Reply to Your Customers for You

The first use of ChatGPT as your customer service rep is pretty obvious: It can reply to your customer questions, queries, reviews, or even complaints for you. If this seems like a scapegoat way of dealing with the messages, well, you're not wrong. But if the scapegoat method proves to be more successful than the original way, and ends up in more satisfied customers while saving you the time and stress of having to reply to these messages yourself, why not use it, I say. You can set up automated emails or get ChatGPT to formulate responses to your customer reviews and complaints by itself. You can also upload your customer reviews and complaints into ChatGPT and prompt it to generate a reply that captures the understanding, empathetic tone that you just don't have it in you to embody that day. Another perk of using ChatGPT to reply to your customers for you is that you can prompt it to write reviews of specific lengths. This is particularly handy for responding to customers on social media, which often has a certain word or character limit.

Improve on Current Customer Service Chatbots

If your company already makes use of chatbots to help out with your customer service needs, then ChatGPT is just another, albeit massively beneficial, upgrade to this system. What are known as "customer-facing chatbots" have been around since the early 2000s. Although these earlier chatbots were helpful in lightening the workload of customer service agents (especially when it came to taking care of frequently asked questions), they were limited to rule-based, pre-programmed responses that relied on a very selective set of keywords or phrases to get results. As such, these chatbots were often inaccurate in their customer responses, and ended up frustrating the person more than helping them out. In this form, chatbots were really limited versions of the Google search function and were very easily confused when processing natural language. Then, ChatGPT came along and changed the game in the accuracy and capacities of chatbots for customer service.

As an LLM, natural language processing (NLP) is part of ChatGPT's game, which means that it doesn't need you to use the exact keyword to get accurate results. As a deep-learning AI, it can also bear in its synthetic mind the previous messages in a thread, making it head and shoulders above any chatbot that came before it. These two factors—its conversation skills and ability to keep in mind the history and context of the conversation—makes ChatGPT the ultimate upgrade to your current customer service chatbots, and only more upgrades are on the horizon. It really is a new dawn for the chatbot industry, and ChatGPT is blazing the trail toward customer service automation.

Summarizing and Translating Customer Inquiries

If you don't trust ChatGPT to directly respond to your customers for you, then another thing you could use it for is to summarize your customer inquiries. If you have a large and active customer base who engages with your company on the regular, then it can become quite overwhelming to stay on top of your customer service game. In the past, you'd have to hire even more people to serve as customer service agents for your business. Now you can just delegate reading customer inquiries and feedback to ChatGPT. Upload your customer inquiries to your one-stop-shop digital customer service agent, and through various prompts, you can get different summarized forms of the dataset. You could ask it to summarize the main points of an individual inquiry or prompt it to organize customer ratings. It could also analyze an entire dataset of customer feedback, highlighting key trends or even generating a report on them, providing insights on how you could improve in the future based on said feedback.

Other than summarizing customer feedback, ChatGPT can help out in customer service by translating customer inquiries. This is especially useful if you run a multinational or online business with a diverse customer base. If you don't currently, maybe ChatGPT can be your way to break into these other markets by not only translating feedback from them to you, but also writing content to be translated from your language to theirs.

Virtual Assistants for All!

As we've seen throughout this book, ChatGPT makes one great virtual assistant. This becomes particularly useful for customer service, as you can create a virtual assistant for your website, for example, streamlining and personalizing your user's experience with your site. Furthermore, ChatGPT also gives each of your employees their very own virtual assistant. It can be fully integrated with most of your organization's existing tools and platforms, from the front-end of customer contact platforms to the back end of scheduling systems. By training your employees on how to get the most out of ChatGPT, you'll be able to improve their productivity tenfold. This makes it a must not only for customer service, but for servicing your organization too.

The Digital Marketer

By its very nature, digital marketing is another industry that has always been on the cutting edge of AI innovation and tech-based automation. According to Mailchimp, digital or online marketing involves "the promotion of brands to connect with potential customers using the internet and other forms of digital communication" (Mailchimp, 2023). If it appears on a phone, iPad, computer, or any other device, then it's a form of digital marketing.

With our world becoming ever more tech-obsessed, digital marketing is increasingly taking over from what is often called "traditional marketing," aka advertising in magazines, on billboards, and the like. If you want to be successful in your marketing campaigns, you need to aim your efforts where they'll be most effective. In other words, you need to market your wares where your target audience hangs out. With 89% of Americans going online on a daily basis, you best be assured that unless you're selling adult diapers, every one of your customers has an online presence of some sort (Mailchimp, 2023). There are a wide variety of different kinds of digital marketing, a few of which we've covered already. These include SEO marketing, content marketing, email marketing, and social media marketing.

Other types of digital marketing include pay-per-click marketing (where you pay for advertising on a site or social media platform only if/when people click on your ads), affiliate marketing (offering people commission if they promote and make sales on behalf of your business), and influencer marketing (similar to affiliate marketing, but where the person that promotes your business is someone with a large following online). In this section, we'll go over the main benefits of digital marketing, before covering how you can leverage ChatGPT to drive sales through enhancing the efficiency and effectiveness of your online advertising efforts.

The Benefits of Quality Digital Marketing

As we've mentioned before, the main aim of a business is to make money. If it's not, then you're either running a charity or have one expensive hobby. In order to make those sweet profits, you need to sell your products or services to customers, and to do that, you need to reach through to them with your quality marketing. Because of the sheer number of people online, it only makes sense to market your wares there. Besides granting your business access to a wider target audience, there are a number of other benefits to setting in place a solid digital marketing plan. Let's go through a list of the top ones before giving you the insider scoop on how to use ChatGPT to further improve the efficiency and effectiveness of your digital marketing efforts.

More Personalized Than Traditional Marketing

The first major benefit of digital marketing is that it allows you to connect with your target audience on a much more personal level than traditional marketing methods allow. This isn't only because your customers see posts from your business show up on their personal social media pages, but also because you can gather much more accurate, specific, and detailed customer data through digital marketing. Through analyzing this data, businesses are better equipped to tailor their digital marketing ads and campaigns, ensuring they reflect what their customers are interested in. You just don't have the data on-hand to do this with traditional marketing, and even if you do manage to get it, it's often inaccurate, or not nearly as detailed or specific as what you gain from analyzing customer data for your digital marketing efforts.

Now, this isn't to say that traditional marketing doesn't work, or that you should allocate all of your marketing budget on the digital side of business life. It's just that, since the birth of social media, we live in a much more "personal" age where people expect to communicate to a business directly (like they were talking to a person), and they also expect that the business "talks" to them directly in the messages it sends out to them too. To make your customer feel special, there's not much better than the personalization offered by digital marketing.

Broaden Your Reach

As the place where people from around the world hang out, the internet is the largest "community" out there. As such, when you post your ad on your website or on one of the social platforms, more people than just those in your local neighborhood or geographical area are going to see it, unless you've specifically limited your post's reach to target that audience. This latter point is another great advantage of digital marketing: You can aim your ads at specific groups of people. This means that you not only broaden your geographic reach through using digital platforms to market your wares, but also further personalize the interactions people have with your company. From macromarketing to the micro, the digital world has you covered!

More Flexible and Easier on the Wallet

Not only does digital marketing help to personalize your ads and expand your reach, but it does so at a lower price than the less-personalized, smaller-audience marketing offered by the traditional route. It's pretty pricey to buy space in a newspaper to place your ad, and even more so if you want to get some TV time to speak to your audience. Not only does traditional marketing generally carry a hefty price tag, but it also takes much of the control over the marketing process out of your hands. Once you submit your ad to the newspaper, radio or TV station, etc., that's that. You have to then sit back and wait for your ad to pop up.

You can't control how many people are watching, reading, or listening to that traditional marketing medium at the precise time your ad strolls through their lives. Add to that, you can't control how they're feeling at that moment they see your ad—are they perusing the newspaper in their lunch break with everything they read soon to be forgotten in the second half of the day, or are they irritated at an ad showing up in the middle of their soapie, or before their new favorite tune on the radio? This makes many of the traditional marketing methods quite static and more "hit-or-miss" than their digital equivalents. On social media, for example, you can use analytics to determine the best time to post your ad based on who your target audience is and when they're most likely to be relaxing and scrolling through the feed. You can then automate your post to be released at this precise time. More than that, because of the nature of social media feeds, your ad will show up on their feeds not once, but for days to come, and because of the nature of the internet, your ad won't be a one-and-done, but remain up forever more. All at a far cheaper price tag than that carried by traditional marketing!

Convenient Conversions and Quantifiable Results

The final main benefit of quality digital marketing is that it's not only more convenient for you, but more convenient for your customers too. As we mentioned above, one of the major drawbacks of traditional marketing is that you can't control when or where your customer sees your ad, and even less how they're feeling when they see it. If they're scrolling through their social media feed on their lunch break and see something they may be interested in, they can save it for later, rather than forgetting about it because of inconvenient timing. This is what we in the marketing biz or in the business biz call convenient conversions: Making it as easy as possible for an interested or potentially interested customer to convert their interest into making an actual purchase. Conversation rates are another great analytic you can gain from digital marketing that is quite tough to determine in traditional marketing.

Besides conversion rates, there are a number of other analytics offered by digital marketing. There is a load of digital marketing software out there that can automatically track how many clicks a blog post gets, how many people visit your home page and how many move on to a different page on your website, and of course, how many people follow through to actually making a purchase. Of course, as we shall see in the next section, ChatGPT can help to streamline your digital marketing for more convenient conversions while also providing detailed analysis of your marketing analytics, and much more!

ChatGPT as Your One-Stop-Shop Digital Marketing House

With the importance of digital marketing outlined, it's time to look at how you can utilize the full power of ChatGPT to serve as your one-stop-shop digital marketer. We've already gone through many of the different means by which ChatGPT can help you produce high-quality content and enhance your organization's communications and customer service, so we're not going to restate that here (although it's important to note that these are essential for getting the most out of your virtual digital marketer that is ChatGPT). Rather than repeat what's already been said, let's add a few more marketing tips and automation tricks to our ever-growing cheatsheet on how to use ChatGPT as your pocket-sized business partner.

Predictive Analytics

As we ended off the previous section speaking about, a major benefit of digital marketing is the ability to gather a load of data about your customers and what's working and what's not in terms of your marketing. A major benefit of using ChatGPT as a digital marketing tool, is that it can then take that data and organize and collate it into analytics known as marketing metrics. These include the conversion rates that we've talked about already, as well as the clickthrough rate, social media engagement, web traffic, subscription rate, and so on. As we covered in our analytics section, ChatGPT can take these marketing analytics and turn them into highlights summaries or marketing reports that make them understandable to the average business owner. With enough data, it can even make insightful recommendations and marketing predictions to help you plan out your next best advertising move.

When it comes to noticing patterns and trends in large volumes of data, we humans don't come close to AI. It's not only able to provide far more detailed analysis of the data, but does it in the time it takes us to power up our computers. Using the data you give it and its generative AI skills, ChatGPT can provide some very insightful and actionable steps forward for your digital marketing efforts. And if you ask it to play the role of a digital marketer, you're sure to get even better results. Remember, to get the most out of ChatGPT, your prompt game needs to be strong.

Marketing Automation

When it comes to running your own business, the more you can delegate to other people the better, because no matter what you do, you're always going to have too much on your plate. Most businesses start as a single person operation or as a small group of people who do everything. Then, as the fledgling business begins to grow, they slowly delegate tasks and roles to others either through partnering with them, hiring them, or paying for their services. When it comes to digital marketing, delegate to ChatGPT.

Whether it be generating a variety of "personalized" emails for a new promotion, or analyzing your previous social media campaign before planning for the next, you can automate these unnecessarily time-consuming marketing roles by getting ChatGPT to take care of them for you!

Audience Research and Development

The next way that ChatGPT can help you with your digital marketing needs is by taking care of that essential business grower: audience research. As we've seen so far, our deep learning chatbot can help you to define your target market, determine their likes and wants, hopes and dreams, and decide on the next best step forward for your company and its marketing campaigns by highlighting what's working and what's not. All of this data gathering and insight generating falls under the umbrella term "audience research." Through researching your audience for you, ChatGPT can help you better understand what they are interested in, how they prefer to see your ads or interact with your company, what their spending habits are, and how you and your product or service can help make their lives that little bit better.

You can use ChatGPT to analyze data related to customer queries, social media interactions, conversion rates, and purchase history. Armed with this info, you'll be perfectly placed to create a killer digital marketing campaign to conquer each and all of your competition, and claim even more of the market share.

Customer Surveys

Linked to audience research and development is the creation of customer surveys. Surveys have always been a key part of a company's marketing plans. In traditional marketing, surveys asking "How did you hear about us?" were pretty much the only way for a business to figure out if their marketing efforts were working, as well as which ones were working better than others. Surveys are also hugely useful in digital marketing as a means to gather feedback from customers and develop insights that can help you to improve your products and/or services, or tweak your marketing strategy to better prime it for success. And using ChatGPT as your digital marketing powerhouse, creating and collating customer surveys has never been easier.

You can use the generative AI, deep learning chatbot to help you create a questionnaire, or organize the layout of your survey, formulated using the latest in survey research. You can get it to produce a list of keywords to use in your questions, or get it to translate your survey into a variety of languages. Finally, you can get ChatGPT to analyze your survey data, and even create a report to highlight the key feedback and findings from the survey it created. All you have to do is prompt ChatGPT on what you want it to do.

Prompts for Your Pocket-sized Business Partner

With digital marketing done, we come to the end of this chapter on how to use ChatGPT as your pocket-sized business partner. As we've seen, our lil' chatbot can do a lot more than just generate content for your company. It can also help to streamline and refine your business communications, analyze your business data, and even service your customers—in terms of digital customer service, that is! Before we move on to the next chapter, there's one thing left to do, and that's to get our prompts on. Let's go over a few prompts for each of the sections we covered in this chapter, helping you to take action right away using ChatGPT as your pocket-sized business partner!

Business Communication

- Write an email informing an employee in X position that they are being offered a promotion to Y position including the following information.
- Create an actionable plan to streamline business communication using ChatGPT.
- Answer the following customer communication using an understanding and empathetic tone, informing them that we cannot provide them with a refund if X.
- Summarize the minutes from a meeting in bullet point form, using full sentences and simple English.
- What is the best way to communicate with suppliers in the X industry?

Data Analytics

- What are the most important analytics or key performance indicators for X industry?

- Analyze the data for our conversion rates and develop a highlights report on the most important trends in the dataset.
- Develop a SWOT analysis for X business based on the following key performance indicators.
- Generate a report on the spending habits of X target market and suggest actionable steps to marketing Y product/service to this target market.
- Play the role of a data analyst working for X esteemed company. Analyze the following dataset on Y and provide constructive and actionable feedback on how to improve Z.

Customer Service

- Generate a list of phrases used by customer service agents to show empathy.
- Act as a customer buying X product. Describe what influences your purchasing decision.
- Create a customer service guide for employees in X industry.
- Make a list of frequently asked questions for X product or service.
- What are common customer service mistakes made by businesses?

Digital Marketing

- Write a post-purchase email for X company selling Y product. Make sure to include the following.

- Generate a list of blog post titles to engage X target audience based on the following topics.
- Act as a digital marketer specializing in X industry. Create a three-month digital marketing campaign based on X topic.
- Act as a social media manager. Create an actionable plan for increasing engagement for X social media platform.
- Make a list of the top keywords for X industry.

As with all good things, this chapter must come to an end. We've covered quite a bit of ground as we went through the ways to use ChatGPT as your pocket-sized business partner. From business analytics to communications, content creation to customer service, ChatGPT has your professional needs covered. But what about your personal needs? We saw in the previous chapter how you can use ChatGPT to assist with your mental health needs, and in the chapter before that how to use it as your very own PA. We're going to carry on with this personal vibe in the next chapter as we move from the office desk to your living room and look into how our deep learning AI can become a part of your everyday life—a roommate, if you will, but with fewer noise complaints!

Chapter 6
A New Roommate, but Less Noisy

The way I see it, there are two ways that our relationship with technology can go. We can either develop a symbiotic relationship with it, incorporating AI throughout our lives—from the professional to the personal—and use it to enhance our life experience and productivity as we teach it how to become better and better, or we can freak out and try to kill the "monster" we've created. If it's the latter, then that's how I think realities painted in movies like *The Terminator* or *The Matrix* come to be. Some food for thought: AI is as good or evil as the person (or people) using it.

With that caveat out of the way, let's begin this chapter on how we can (safely and effectively) incorporate ChatGPT into our daily routines and even let it move into your house with you. The best part of this roommate is that you don't actually have to see them, hear them, or give over any of your personal space to them! If you've already made the move toward smart homes, then ChatGPT is just another AI roommate helping you to keep at the peak of your game.

In this chapter, we're going to "flex" ChatGPT's skillset as we see how versatile this lil' deep learning chatbot really is, extending from the business world into your home. We'll look at how ChatGPT can be used to help you complete personal tasks, achieve goals, and streamline your daily routines. After that, we'll go over some important steps to take to ensure your privacy and safety when interacting with AI tools like ChatGPT because, like with any roommate, you've got to set your boundaries.

Your AI Roommate

With the versatility of generative AI combined with deep learning technology, ChatGPT can do far more than just answer customer queries or help to analyze and refine your business processes. It can also help you to streamline, or even automate, many of your day-to-day tasks and routines too. Whether it's managing your personal email, setting reminders for family member's birthdays, penciling Tinder dates into your calendar, or drafting your shopping lists, ChatGPT has you covered. It can even help to make you the most informed and knowledgeable person in the room through summarizing books or curating news for you. In other words, ChatGPT can help to take you up a few pegs in the social ladder and have you performing at the top of your game.

Incorporating ChatGPT Into Your Daily Life

Since its release in 2022, ChatGPT has taken the world by storm. Its ability to enhance the effectiveness, efficiency, and productivity of those that use it has revolutionized the way that we work, as well as the way we market our products and services. Remember that Microsoft's founder Bill Gates places ChatGPT second on his list of technological advancements of his lifetime. And no, he doesn't place Microsoft as number one, although there are interesting correlations between what Windows managed with operating systems and what ChatGPT is bringing about with virtual AI assistants. That is, both instantly became "must-haves" in the realms of both business and personal life. Whether OpenAI's creation comes to enjoy the same depth and breadth of reach that Microsoft has accomplished remains to be seen. But in my opinion, it's just a matter of time. Let's go through some of the main ways that you can start using ChatGPT to improve your personal life today.

Automate Repetitive Tasks

As we've mentioned in the previous chapter, time is one of the most, if not *the most*, of important resources that we've got. It's also one that we have less and less of each day, each hour, each minute, each second. The only way we can "make" more of the stuff is to streamline our routines by getting rid of things that aren't worth the time they take up, or increasingly, by delegating certain repetitive and automatable tasks to technology. We used to have to wash our own clothes until the washing machine was invented, we used to have to reheat food in the oven until the microwave was invented, and before the oven, we used to have to make a fire to cook our food.

Over the years, delegating tasks to technology has become the name of the game as we try to get the most out of the time we have taking part in the human race. Think of ChatGPT as the next great automizer of repetitive tasks; taking care of things such as scheduling your appointments, sending out invitations or reminders, writing birthday messages or "thank you" emails, or even helping you to plan out meals (it can't cook for you yet, but I'm sure the tech will be released soon!). All of this is done so that you can focus on what you value most in life without having to sweat the small stuff.

Learn New Things

With ChatGPT, we now have even more information at our fingertips than ever before. Well, we have the same amount of info rather, but it's easier to understand and simpler to consume than ever before. If you have a question you've always wanted answered, are looking to up your general knowledge for your next quiz night, or just want to stay informed on the latest goings-on and trends in the world, ChatGPT's got you covered. More than that, if you've ever wanted to learn a new language, it's never been easier with the help of ChatGPT. You can ask our chatbot for helpful language learning pointers, ask it to create a list of exercises to improve your skills, and even have a conversation with you. If you type a prompt into ChatGPT in the language you're learning, then ChatGPT will reply to you in that language.

Simplify Large Tasks

Have a wedding to plan or a large personal goal that you want to accomplish? It can be quite overwhelming to begin working on such big and complex tasks, let alone to successfully complete them. Luckily, you now have your very own personal assistant ready and waiting to help you achieve any task, no matter how big or small, simple or complex. ChatGPT can help you by breaking down massive personal projects into manageable chunks, creating a budget or plan of action for going forward, researching venues, times, and prime dates, or even writing invitations for your guests. No matter what personal project you're looking to complete, ChatGPT is ready and waiting to help you achieve it. Remember though, our deep learning chatbot is only as helpful as your prompt is accurate. So make sure that you've worked out exactly what you want to achieve, and word your task for ChatGPT clearly and carefully. If you want to complete the project within a certain timeframe, make sure that you let ChatGPT know. If there are certain checkpoints or other measurable milestones for your task, include them in the info you give your personal PA. Finally, if any steps are unclear or confusing, or if you need clarification, then feel free to let the chatbot know—it might be great at helping you achieve your goals, but it's not necessarily going to get it perfect the first time. And remember, the more you chat to the bot in a thread, the more accurate it becomes!

Search the Web in Style

Google has dominated the search engine game for a good while now. If you wanted to find out some tidbit of info from the past

10 years or so, most people would tell you, "Just Google it!" to find the answer you seek. In fact, "Google it" has become such a common phrase that in 2006, the term was added to the Oxford English Dictionary (The Decision Lab, 2023). There is even a growing body of research that shows Google has changed the way we humans remember things. Called "the Google Effect" or "digital amnesia," the theory shows that we are far less likely to commit things to memory if we know how to find the info online. What we remember rather, is where to find the info we're after. While this may seem like a scary thing at first, it's not really anything new. Our memories changed when we started writing things down, and again when we invented the printing press. It also frees up a lot of our brain space to remember things that are actually important, rather than those things we can easily find online. Now with the invention of ChatGPT, the way we search for the information we're after is changing once again. We don't have to scrounge through a miasma of websites to find what we're looking for; all we have to do is enter the right prompt into our nifty lil' chatbot and it will do the grunt work for us. Not only that, but it can even condense said info into a handy summary to save you even more time and brain power. Talk about a convenient way to surf the web!

Plan Out Many Aspects of Your Life

Whether you're looking to plan a trip, plan your day, or get on top of the plan for your life, ChatGPT's got you covered. In terms of travel plans, our digital PA can help you by creating the ideal itinerary for your journey; providing a list of accommodation options, a day-by-day playbook of sights to see and local cuisines to try, as well as sorting out travel routes and transportation options too. It can also provide you with a number of different kinds of itineraries; depending on if you're a fan of adventure holidays off the beaten track, relaxing weekends away, or are more of an urban jungle kind of traveler. It can also help you to research the cultural customs of your holiday location and even provide you with a list of useful phrases in the local lingo.

If such holiday planning seems a world away from your busy day-to-day, let ChatGPT help you to finesse that too. Our chatbot allows you to streamline your productivity, manage your time effectively, and prepare yourself for successfully carpe diem-ing each and every day! You can ask ChatGPT for time management tips and techniques to help you organize and prioritize your to-do list, write memos and reminders, and even reflect on your progress today while also discussing ways to improve on it for tomorrow.

More than just travel plans and daily to-do's, ChatGPT can also help you to plan out pretty much all aspects of your life. It does this through helping you to set your goals, identify measurable milestones on your path to success, and providing feedback on how to overcome any obstacles that pop up on the way to you living the life of your dreams. It can even provide you with advice on which option to choose when you reach a crossroad, be your accountability manager, and give you some much needed motivation when you require it most.

Role-Playing and Other Kinds of Fun

As we've seen in this chapter and in previous ones, one of the most groundbreaking things that ChatGPT can do is to take on pretty much any perspective or play any role that you can think of. You can ask the deep learning AI to role-play an interior designer and provide you with a plan to spruce up your living room, to act as an editor and provide you with constructive feedback on that novel you've been working on, or even to take on the persona of a math tutor to help your kids with their homework. Besides the serious side of role-playing, you can also use this feature to have some fun! You could ask ChatGPT to "play" a historical figure or your favorite book character for you to have a chat with, for example. OpenAI's revolutionary LLM is the most fun you can have with role-playing (outside of the bedroom, that is!).

Besides role-playing there are also many more fun uses of ChatGPT. You could ask the chatbot to tell you a joke, to ask you a riddle, or even to act as a quizmaster and create a bunch of trivia challenges for your next dinner party. It can even create a playlist of songs to reflect your current mood or to uplift it, write poetry, and discuss hypotheticals or "what-if" scenarios with you.

Safeguarding Your Space

I'm sure you can now see what a useful and entertaining "roommate" ChatGPT can be. But just like with any roomie, you need to make sure that you still protect your privacy and ensure your safety while sharing the same space. In this section, we're going to discuss the importance of privacy and safety when interacting with AI tools like ChatGPT. We'll go over the fail safes that Open AI has put in place to ensure your personal data is protected and anonymized while using their LLM, before giving you a list of do's and don'ts related to maintaining your privacy and protecting your sensitive personal information.

Ensuring Your Privacy When Using ChatGPT

We've talked a lot so far on how you can use ChatGPT to improve your own life, both in terms of the professional and personal. But it's important to remember that besides time, nothing in life is a one-way street, especially not something that's free. Remember earlier in the book when we mentioned that OpenAI "trained" its deep learning LLM on a massive dataset of 570 gigs? Well, the question then becomes: Where did all this info—amassing to around 300 billion words—come from? The answer: Whatever OpenAI could scrounge together from ebooks, research articles, website content, blog posts, and any other easily obtainable data that the company could get its hands on—without getting in too much trouble for doing so. This sometimes included personal information obtained without the consent of the person too.

The bottom line is that in order for a large language model like ChatGPT to function and improve, it needs to be fed as much data as possible. The more data that it is trained on, the more accurate it will be in answering your prompts, and the more capable it will be of determining what text it should generate next based on that. This leads to the big catch-22 of the

ChatGPT movement: The tech can help to make us more efficient and productive than ever before, but it can come at the cost of our privacy to make this happen. It's important to keep in mind that ChatGPT is not only trained on data obtained from businesses or academia, but also on content created by average Joes like me and you. There is no way to know whether your data was used in the chatbot's dataset or what kind of personal info it was fed, nor is there at present any way to delete your personal information from ChatGPT.

Europe, which leads the world in laws and regulations protecting the personal data of its citizens, has a policy in place called the General Data Protection Regulation (GDPR for short). The GDPR aims to protect the personal info of the 400 million odd people across Europe through regulating the data that organizations can collect and store, as well as regulating how they can use the personal data they obtain. And, unlike the privacy rules and regulations in the U.S. (which are enforced on a state level rather than across the continent), the European GDPR applies even if someone's personal info is readily available online. In other words, just because a company can publicly access someone's information doesn't mean said company can do whatever they want with it. This puts Europe at heads with the privacy policies of many of the largest tech and social media companies in the world, and of course, with OpenAI too.

The first country in Europe to open legal proceedings against OpenAI's use of personal information in ChatGPT's dataset was Italy. According to the Italian regulator, Garante per la Protezione dei Dati Personali, OpenAI had no legal right to access and use the personal information it found on the internet. As such, in March 2023, Italy's Garante issued what it called a "temporary emergency decision" demanding that OpenAI cease using the private data of its citizens, listing four ways in which ChatGPT violated the regulations put in place by GDPR. The first was to do with a lack of age restrictions enforced by ChatGPT, both in terms of the data it collected and in terms of having no age control over who could use the generative AI (or what they could use it for). The second stated issue dealt with ChatGPT's inability to ensure that the information it collected about people was accurate, and the third to do with the fact that people were never informed that their data was being used in the LLM's dataset. The final argument put forward by Garante was that OpenAI had "no legal basis" for using people's personal information to train its creation (Burgess, 2023). Mere days after Italy announced that it was conducting a probe into ChatGPT for these reasons, other European countries joined in too, with Germany, Ireland, and France requesting that Garante share their findings with their own data regulators so that they could take similar action. OpenAI's response to the Italian probe? They stated they were investigating the claims and would provide an official response once Garante's investigation was complete. Then they blocked Italians from being able to access and use ChatGPT.

Any great innovation or new technology comes with a significant amount of risk, both for its creators and its users, and ChatGPT is no different. Many tech experts believe that OpenAI's chatbot marks a tipping point for artificial intelligence and the way we use it, as well as the way it "uses" us.

Generative AI has the ability to revolutionize the way we work, learn, and live in the tech-obsessed world we've created, but there does need to be a balancing act between risk and reward. Also important to remember, is that OpenAI is not a charity or some philanthropic venture; it's a for-profit business. While we do not (presently) pay to use ChatGPT, nor did OpenAI pay for the data it used to train its LLM. Nobody has been compensated for the use of their data, while OpenAI's worth has doubled since 2021, with the company being valued at around $29 billion in 2023 (Gal, 2023). Add to that OpenAI's release of ChatGPT Plus in February 2023, a paid-for subscription version of its AI that prioritizes users and guarantees them ongoing access to the platform, and you've got a perfect storm of a data privacy conundrum. ChatGPT Plus is expected to generate revenue of over $1 billion by 2024 (Gal, 2023).

So, how can you ensure your privacy when using ChatGPT? Or is it even possible to do so? While deleting your personal info from the chatbot's dataset doesn't seem likely, there are ways that you can ensure you use ChatGPT as safely and securely as possible.

Don't Share Sensitive Information

ChatGPT is not the first technological advancement that inspires fears over personal information, nor will it be the last. We live in an increasingly interconnected and internet-connected world, and doing so comes at a price more costly than money: It comes at the price of our privacy. In the modern world, it's not only businesses or celebrities that are easy to find online, but almost anyone (who hasn't been living under a rock or on a deserted island for the past 20 years) is an easy Google search or social media stalk away from being found by anyone, anywhere around the world. Most of us have not only accepted this fact, but have embraced the lifestyle with full force, posting constant updates on what we're doing and where we're doing it so that our adoring followers can follow our rose-tinted journey through life. These followers aren't just our friends and family either, but can be complete strangers that we'll never see or actually speak to in our lives. Some of these unknowns may try and strike up a conversation with us, sending emails or sliding into our DMs, not to connect or share in our joy and happiness, but rather to try and gain access to our sensitive personal information to use for their own nefarious means. This is called phishing, and is one of the most serious and dire consequences of our interconnected world.

Although it may be mean to lump ChatGPT in with these modern-day "phishermen and women," it helps to think about our generative AI chatbot in the same way when it comes to the sensitive data and personal information you provide it with. Just like you wouldn't send anyone your passwords, banking details, etc., so too should you not enter them into the prompts you write for ChatGPT. Steer clear of including intellectual property or trade secrets in them too. It's important to remember that whatever info you share with ChatGPT gets added into its ever-growing dataset, and because ChatGPT's data bank is in the public domain, your private info will become accessible to the general public too.

The bottom line is that ChatGPT records your conversations. So any personal info, uploaded files, or prompt threads you enter into the chatbot are there to stay. After getting a lot of backlash about the cybersecurity risk that ChatGPT potentially poses due to this, OpenAI has added some ways that you can retain at least a certain degree of control over your privacy when using their chatbot. If you go to settings in ChatGPT and scroll down to data controls, you'll find something called "chat history and training." If you disable this, then the chat history you have with the generative AI won't be recorded. This feature was introduced in April 2023, and marks a large step by OpenAI to try and help you remain safe and secure while using their software. However, even if you disable this feature, it's still not recommended to share any personal or sensitive info with the chatbot.

Delete Your Conversations After Use

Have you heard of the term "burn after reading" before? This phrase applies to spies, and now to ChatGPT. Disabling chat history and training is a great first step to ensuring your safety and privacy when using OpenAI's deep learning chatbot, but it may not be enough. This function stops ChatGPT from being trained on the info you enter into it, but it doesn't actually delete it. This means that, should there be a data breach, your chat history could still be leaked. This happened in March 2023, when a "bug" entered the ChatGPT system from an open-source library that was added to its data bank, leading to users being able to see the titles of other users' chat history. Scarier still, some payment information from 1.2% of ChatGPT Plus users became accessible to all, including their names, email addresses, and even credit card information (Kan, 2023). This may seem like a tiny fraction of the total number of ChatGPT users, but if you were one of the unlucky ones to have their personal info leaked, then the fact that 98.8% of other people remained safe means little to nothing to you.

To ensure that you remain better protected from such data breaches, you can delete your chat history after each use of the chatbot. While this may not protect your credit card info (sorry ChatGPT Plus users), it does ensure that others won't be able to gain access to your chat history titles should another such bug or breach happen in the future. To delete your chat history, go to settings and, under "general," you'll find the "clear" button. This will clear all conversations you've had with ChatGPT. While this is an effective way to keep your chat history safe, it can also mean that you have to start "training" the deep learning chatbot from scratch every time you begin a conversation, which sort of kills ChatGPT's ability to generate more accurate and personalized results the more you chat with it. This can be particularly frustrating if you work on larger projects with ChatGPT that take more than one session to complete. If this is what you use ChatGPT for, then there is another option. You can view, select, and delete individual conversation threads, allowing you to clear your chat history on a project-by-project basis, rather than after every time you use the chatbot. To do this, go to your list of conversations on the ChatGPT platform and click on the specific chats that you want to delete. Then, click on the trash can icon to remove these from your (and ChatGPT's) data bank.

Anonymize Your Data

If you need to keep your chat history for prolonged periods of time and over a number of different projects, then the above method is not going to work very well for you. In this case, you can make use of what we in the IT biz call data anonymization techniques. Through using these techniques, you can keep the insights ChatGPT gains from your previous chats while still protecting your personal information, and preventing potential bugs or hacks leaking your or your customer's identities. There are a number of different ways to do this, and although they don't guarantee that your chat history and conversation threads won't be leaked, they can help to make this data useless to anyone besides yourself. According to the Personal Data Protection Commission of Singapore, here are some of the best ways to anonymize your data (Lim, 2023):

1. Suppress Unnecessary Attributes

In attribute suppression, you remove any pieces of information that aren't essential for your results. To see how this works, let's use the example of customer spending patterns. In order to get accurate results from ChatGPT in this regard, you'll need to feed it the amount that your individual customers spent, as well as the dates they made purchases. You don't, however, need to upload your customers' names, banking details, and so on to gain accurate results. It may take a bit more work on your end to separate the required data from the personal info, but this ensures that you and your customers remain safe and secure should something go awry in OpenAI's systems, and is still a lot quicker than you doing the entire process without using the LLM.

2. Be Wise, Pseudonize

While uploading the actual names of people in your prompts is a big no, this doesn't mean that you have to leave out these attributes completely. Rather, you can provide pseudonyms for names and keep an offline list of who the different pseudo-names refer to. An example of how this could work would be to use numbers to represent your customers, patients, students, employees, etc. So, instead of Bob, Jim, and Sally, you could have Employee One, Employee Two, Employee Three.

3. Data Perturbation

Linked to "pseudonizing" the names you enter into ChatGPT, is perturbating the data set. This means purposefully modifying the numbers and amounts you enter into your prompt, keeping an offline record of how much you modified the figures in the dataset by. Let's say that you want to find out what the average age of your customers is, or want to record the ages of your students or patients. Rather than entering their actual age, you can modify this by a certain number, either adding or subtracting years from it. Then, once ChatGPT has collated the age data, you can add or subtract this difference to get an accurate answer for yourself while ensuring the actual age of your students or patients is incorrect in ChatGPT's dataset.

With your space safeguarded and protective measures put in place, you're now ready to embrace your new roommate with full power! And what a powerhouse of productivity and assistive prowess ChatGPT can be when used to its fullest (and safest) potential. So far in this book, we've learned how to welcome ChatGPT into our lives, covering both the personal and the professional sides. But we've only just dipped our toes into the waters of what we can use this revolutionary deep learning chatbot for. In the next chapter, we're going to venture beyond the shallows and dive deeper into advanced applications, exploring the real power of this innovative new AI. Let's push ChatGPT to its (mildly sarcastic) limit!

Chapter 7
Pushing ChatGPT to Its (Mildly Sarcastic) Limit

As I'm sure you've more than started to see, the only limits of ChatGPT are the ones that you set yourself. As we covered in the previous chapter, it's vital to put in place these safeguards, and to know how to protect yourself from potential privacy risks and data leaks, as you need to do with any tech in the modern age. But once you've protected yourself, why not see how far you can push it or use it to improve your life? In this chapter, we're going to go past the ordinary to cover the extraordinary as we explore some advanced applications and potential future improvements in the pipework for this revolutionary new technology.

Power Tools

While ChatGPT generates text in human language, this is not all that it can be used for. For example, as we shall see in this section, ChatGPT can be quite the coder too. It can assist with many programming tasks, such as code generation and bug detection. It's important to remember that, as extraordinary as our lil' chatbot may be, it's not perfect. As such, just like you would do a human edit of any text that it generates for you, so should you double, or even triple-check, any code that it generates for you too. One other great thing that ChatGPT can be is your very own personal coding tutor. In fact, as we shall see in the second part of this section, coding is not the only thing that ChatGPT can tutor you in; it can be quite the language teacher too! But before we get to this power tool use of ChatGPT, let's first look into how you can use it to redefine your coding life.

A Programmer's Dream

The first advanced "power tool" use of ChatGPT is to use the generative AI to write code for you. As an LLM, ChatGPT's core function is to generate text. As we have seen, it can do this in a large variety of ways and also for a vast array of different languages. These languages aren't only the ones spoken by us humans though, but also includes those "spoken" by machines. This makes the chatbot a powerful tool for software developers and computer programmers. While English is the chatbot's lingua franca, it's also pretty fluent in many of the most popular coding languages out there, such as C#, Java, JavaScript, Python, and PHP (Israelsen, 2023). While it's not guaranteed to get it perfect, especially not for more complex coding projects, it can be an extremely useful tool to assist with generating, optimizing, and completing code. More than that, ChatGPT can also be a coding tutor, helping you to learn programming languages from the ground up.

To use ChatGPT as your coding tool, all you have to do is enter the right prompt into the chatbot. Make sure that you clarify what programming language you want it to generate for you and accurately describe what you want the code to do, using the same natural language as you would if you were prompting the chatbot to generate a blog post for you, for example. ChatGPT will then read your prompt written in English, interpret it, and produce a code snippet that, to its knowledge, meets your requirements. As you can see, with ChatGPT on your side, English really is the new coding language! Once ChatGPT has generated the requested code, you can then copy it from the conversion thread and paste it where needed. More than that, you can also ask ChatGPT to give you a play-by-play account of what the different parts of the code mean and how to use it or enter it into your website, let's say. This is very helpful for coding noobs and can make programming accessible. In fact, when compared to the abilities of human programmers and coders to explain what the code means, ChatGPT can often do a better job, using simple to understand language, and do so with a lot more patience to boot.

While you can use ChatGPT to write code for you, the verdict is still out on whether or not you should let it take over your coding workload for you. As with anything, there are both pros and cons to using ChatGPT as your one-stop coding shop. One of the main benefits is the speed at which ChatGPT can generate code snippets for you to use. It also gets the syntax ("sentence" structure) of the code right more often than not, making it better than the run-of-the-mill programmer you usually hire to do the job for you. This can save you a lot of headaches in runtime errors that humans make when we're writing code from scratch. Added to that, ChatGPT has a vast database of coding expertise from a wide variety of programming backgrounds. This means that it can offer more innovative solutions to coding problems that us single-brained, "solo-perspectived" humans may not have thought of or even know about.

In terms of the drawbacks of using ChatGPT to write code for you, they're the same ones that we've covered in previous chapters: It's not going to be 100% accurate all the time and can lack the contextual knowledge or creativity that human coders bring to the table. Worse still, ChatGPT won't let you know that it doesn't know what it's doing. Like the staunchest narcissist, ChatGPT will adamantly claim to be correct even when it's wrong, and when it finally admits that it may have perhaps, maybe, made a mistake, it will do so bluntly, often without offering a way to rectify the mistake it made. This means that you have to check the code that the chatbot generates for you, test it out, and debug if and when needed, just like you would with code written by a human. Furthermore, ChatGPT also struggles to see the bigger picture of where the code fits into your overall project and what you want to use this specific coding snippet for. It doesn't know the list of best practices and company conventions that you could easily convey to a human coder, and can't determine how the code it generates will interact with other code in the project. Finally, there's no blaming ChatGPT should things go awry with the code it generates for you; when things go tits up, the responsibility falls squarely on you and not some scapegoat freelance programmer.

With the pros and cons of using ChatGPT as your programming assistant defined, it's now time to go through a step-by-step guide on how to use the chatbot to write code for you.

Step 1: Select Your Programming Language

First up in using ChatGPT as your assistant code writer, is to decide on what programming language you want it to write in. As we mentioned earlier, OpenAI's advanced LLM is fluent in many of the most popular coding languages out there. Whether it's Java, Python, or PHP, ChatGPT can code it for you, you just have to tell it what you need.

Step 2: Word Your Prompt Carefully

As we already know, with ChatGPT, the more specific you are with your prompt, the more accurate your results will be. This is particularly prevalent when it comes to getting the chatbot to write code for you. Remember that the prompt language that ChatGPT works best with isn't some coding language, but English. This means that while the chatbot generates code for you in the programming language you need, you should provide it with instructions in clear, grammatically correct, syntactically accurate, English. Besides making sure you use correct wording and sentence structure, also ensure that you provide ChatGPT with as much context as possible. This is particularly important for coding snippets required as part of larger coding projects, or if an understanding of a particular framework is needed to customize the code for your specific requirements. Finally, if the code you're after needs to have a specified input or output format, such as an integer for numbers or a specific radius for a circle, make sure you include this too.

Step 3: Review, Optimize, and Debug as Needed

Once you've got your ChatGPT-generated code, you're ready to copy and paste it into your project. But before you do so, make sure to give that code snippet a lil' review first—ChatGPT's not perfect, after all! And if your coding knowledge is next to non-existent, don't worry! Because our nifty chatbot can help you with that too. You can ask ChatGPT to explain the code that it wrote for you in simple English, ask it to provide a list of ways to review such a code, or even review its own code snippet for you. You can prompt the chatbot to provide suggestions on how to optimize the code it generated for you, enhancing its performance, or improving its readability and efficiency. Remember that the longer the conversation thread goes on, the more accurate ChatGPT becomes! If the code the chatbot generated for you doesn't work when you copy it over, you can also ask ChatGPT to debug it for you, providing a list of potential fixes or ways to improve it.

Coding Prompts

And there you have it! A guide on how to use ChatGPT as your perfect coding assistant defined, outlined, and refined. Before we move on to the next section, let's go over a list of useful prompts you can use to get the most out of the code generator supreme that is ChatGPT (LearnPrompt.org, 2023):

▷ **Prompts for Writing New Code**

- Generate a function in X programming language to perform Y task.
- Write a code in W language to complete X task, taking in Y input variables and returning Z outputs, taking into account the following constraints.
- Code an algorithm in X language to solve Y problem.
- Implement X language script to connect to Y database and execute Z operation.
- Develop X language program to read Y file, perform Z operation, and write results to the following output format.

▷ **Prompts for Reviewing and Debugging Code**

- Identify bugs in the following code snippet written in X programming language.
- Find potential errors with X language code snippet and provide actionable solutions.
- Review X language function for performance issues when processing Y data type.
- Debug X language code: [enter coding snippet]. It should be performing Y function, but instead it's producing Z. Analyze and provide solutions.
- Analyze X language script for potential bugs. The code must process Y data type with Z output types.

▷ **Prompts for Optimizing and Improving Code**

- Provide a list of suggestions on how to optimize X language function: [enter code snippet].
- How can I improve the efficiency of X language code snippet?
- Optimize X language function to perform Y task when handling Z data size while still maintaining the code's speed and accuracy.
- The following code for X programming language is running slower than it should. Please provide actionable ways to refine the code.
- Analyze the following code snippet and provide a more efficient alternative.

▷ **Prompts for Learning Code**

- Please explain what the following code function for X language does.
- Help me to learn the basics of X programming language for Y purpose.
- Provide a step-by-step guide on how to write code for X purpose.
- What is the best programming language to use for Y purpose?
- How can I figure out what's wrong with the following code snippet: [enter code snippet]? Explain it as if you were speaking to a person with no coding experience.

Language Learning Supreme

Besides teaching you how to code, ChatGPT can also be a powerful tool to learn other kinds of languages too. As we've mentioned before, although the LLM's mother tongue is English, LLM is fluent in many other languages. Not only that, but if you word your prompts right, the chatbot can be very good at explaining things in simple, easily understandable ways, and has more patience than even the most zen of teachers. Now, it's important to note that while ChatGPT can understand and generate responses in a large number of languages, even switching or translating between languages with relative ease and surprising accuracy, it is more proficient in some languages than others. This is because, as with everything else, ChatGPT relies on the info that it's got in its 570 gig dataset for its language teaching skills. So, for the more widely spoken languages like English, Spanish, and Mandarin, ChatGPT has a lot of data available on them and can therefore generate detailed and accurate content to help you learn them. But if you're looking to learn languages that are less readily available on the internet (and therefore feature less in ChatGPT's dataset), such as Mongolian or Swahili, for example, you're going to want to find yourself a human tutor.

In a similar vein, ChatGPT doesn't do well with teaching different dialects of a language. So, while you can use it to practice Modern Standard Arabic, you won't be able to use it to hone any of the many dialects of the Arabic language, which can contain quite different grammar, vocabulary, and pronunciation rules. Besides these shortcomings, OpenAI's deep learning LLM can make an excellent tool for improving your second language proficiencies.

Learn New Vocabulary

The first great use of ChatGPT as your go-to language-learning tool is to learn new vocabulary words. You can ask the chatbot to generate word lists on specific topics, graded to your specific level of language learning. Added to that, you can also ask it to use said vocab words in example sentences so that you can practice using them in specific contexts or in different tenses. You can prompt the chatbot to quiz you on your vocabulary, ask it to provide corrections for incorrect spelling, or to generate a list of helpful pronunciation tips. Finally, using ChatGPT's translation abilities, you can ask it to translate words from your native language into the one you're currently learning, or even translate entire sentences for you to practice the vocabulary you're learning in context.

Practice Your Conversation Skills

Learning a new language is about a lot more than just memorizing lists of words though. You need to be able to use said vocabulary in context when conversing to other speakers of the lingo. Practicing your conversation skills can be quite a tough thing to do, especially when you're just starting out, or if you don't have easy access to native speakers of the language. Luckily, ChatGPT is here to help you out with that! And, if you're thinking that ChatGPT can only help you out with written conversation practice, let me put your worries at ease, for there's a voice control plug-in you can integrate into the software to practice your speaking conversation skills too. This plugin allows you to speak your prompts out rather than writing them down, and also provides ChatGPT with the ability to reply audibly too.

Called "Voice Control for ChatGPT," the plugin supports more than 30 languages and allows you to to practice your conversation skills in a much more natural and interactive way by enabling you to actually chat to the bot! Remember that this is on the cutting edge of what ChatGPT can currently do, and so don't get hung up if it makes a mistake or two. Also keep in mind when practicing your conversation skills with ChatGPT that (as of writing) its knowledge of current affairs is limited to September 2021, so don't expect it to converse with you on the latest news or world developments. If you do want it to chat to you about anything that comes after 2021, then make sure to begin the conversation thread by uploading an article or two about the conversation topic. This will also help ChatGPT to provide you with more accurate results for your language conversation practice needs. And don't forget about the "act as" or role-play function of the chatbot, where you can tell it to take on a vast variety of different personas, further tailoring the conversations that you have with it in the language you're learning.

Hone Your Grammar

Besides learning new vocabulary or practicing your speaking skills, ChatGPT can also help you to get your head around that tricky thing called grammar. For most of us, when we hear this word, we're immediately transported back to our school days, back to that dusty, stifling classroom, with an irate teacher snapping commands while the rest of the class sniggers at us not knowing the answer to a question. But learning grammar doesn't have to be that way, not now that ChatGPT is on your side.

Your new digital grammarian can help you to practice your sentence structures, explain the reasoning behind different grammatical forms or when to use specific tenses, and provide constructive feedback on any grammatical errors you make in a patient, non-judgmental way that your school grammar teacher could never achieve. You can also ask the chatbot to generate a range of grammar context-based activities and exercises for you to practice your newly learnt sentence structures and tense forms, because when it comes to grammar, practicing in the right context is key. Examples of grammar worksheets you could prompt ChatGPT to create include fill-in-the-blank exercises, word order activities such as "unjumble the sentence," or dialogue practice focusing on certain grammar rules. You could also ask the chatbot to generate a paragraph or two containing the grammatical structures you're learning so that you can review them in context.

Practice All Four Language Skills

When it comes to learning a language, there are four core skills that you need to focus on. These are reading, writing, listening, and speaking. So far, we've seen how we can use ChatGPT to improve your speaking skills through helping you to practice your conversational prowess and perfect your pronunciation. But the deep-learning LLM can also help you to hone the other three language learning skills too. To help you with your reading, ChatGPT can generate text in the language you are learning, provide definitions to any words that you don't know the meaning to, and even generate comprehension questions based on said reading. If you'd rather use articles you find online, all you have to do is copy and paste them into the conversation thread. You can then prompt the chatbot to explain anything you don't understand the meaning to, or to produce a list of exercises based on the article you uploaded. Rather than copying and pasting the text of the article, you can also try to just enter the link into your prompt, but this doesn't always work and sometimes the chatbot will tell you that it can't read said link. If this happens, then you'll have to copy and paste the text over manually.

If you want to practice your listening skills rather than your reading, then all you need to do is use the voice control plugin we mentioned when chatting about how to use the LLM to improve your conversation skills. Then it can read the articles to you, still providing comprehension questions. Another way to use ChatGPT to improve your listening skills is by generating summaries of YouTube videos for you. To do this, all you need to do is download the extension called "ChatGPT for YouTube," but keep in mind that this only works for videos that have transcripts available. This is hugely useful for language learning, as you can read the summary before watching the video, ensuring that you know what's coming up and that you at least understand the gist of the video. This allows you to better follow what's going on and to improve your listening skills through watching videos slightly above your current level.

Finally, in terms of improving your writing in the language you're learning, you can enter a sentence or two into ChatGPT and ask it to evaluate it for errors, providing comments and corrections to help you improve. You can also begin a written conversation with the chatbot, writing a sentence and prompting it to reply with a question or statement based on what you entered.

Personalized Exercises and Customized Curriculum

The final way that ChatGPT can serve as your powerful tool for language learning is by creating personalized exercises and activities on almost any topic you can think of. You could even begin by prompting the chatbot to provide you with a list of topics, or ask it to generate a list of different kinds of activities based on the pedagogical knowledge it has in its database (which is pretty substantial). Remember, though, the more complicated the worksheet you ask ChatGPT to generate for you, the more likely it is to make mistakes.

Linked to asking the chatbot what the best exercises or activities to use for language learning are, is to ask it to create you a step-by-step plan to learn said language itself. You could ask it what you should focus on at different stages or levels of language learning, or ask it to create a schedule switching between the four language skills based on how much time you have set aside to study and practice. You could even ask it to generate you a personalized curriculum to take you through from beginner to intermediate, and all the way to advanced!

Language Learning Prompts

With ChatGPT, the sky's the limit when it comes to learning a new language. Let's now go over a list of useful prompts for you to use to enhance your language learning and take you from a single lingo zero to a polyglot speaking hero!

▷ **Prompts for Practicing Speaking**

- Provide a list of helpful pronunciation tips for X language.
- How do I say the following sentence in X language?
- Act as my [enter language] conversation partner. Only reply in X language, keeping your answers to Y level of proficiency and speaking on the following topic: [enter topic in the required language].
- What are some common expressions for X language in Y location? Use full sentences written in X language, and provide English explanations for each.
- Act as my [enter language] tutor. Provide a list of conversation exercises for Y level to help me improve my speaking skills.

▷ **Prompts for Practicing Grammar**

- How do I use [enter grammatical form] in X language?
- Write a paragraph containing [enter sentence structure] for X language set at Y level.
- Act as my [enter language] tutor. Provide me with a list of grammar exercises to practice [enter grammar you're looking to learn] for X language at Y level.

- Analyze the following sentence written in X language and identify any grammatical errors that you find. If any grammatical errors are found, provide explanations of the errors.
- Create a list of the common grammatical structures for X language and provide example sentences for each based at Y level, giving the English translation for each, too.

▷ **Prompts for Practicing Reading and Listening**

- Provide a short paragraph written in X language at Y level based on Z topic.
- Generate a list of comprehension questions for the following article graded at X level.
- How can I improve my reading/listening skills, specifically for X language?
- Create a list of reading topics for X language at Y level.
- What online websites are there that provide free listening exercises for X language?

▷ **Prompts for Practicing Writing**

- Act as my [enter language] tutor. Analyze the following paragraph I wrote in X language, providing corrections where errors are found.
- What are some tips for improving my writing in the X language?
- Act as my [enter language] pen pal. Read the following letter I wrote and then write a letter in response.

- Act as my [enter language] tutor. Read the following sentence, providing corrections where necessary before asking a follow-up question.
- Provide 10 exercise questions to help me practice writing in X language at Y level.

The Art of the Impossible

We've seen in this chapter how we can push the boundaries of the powerful tool called ChatGPT by using it to write code or teach you a new language. Carrying on with that vibe, we're now going to push past the more structured, critical uses of this revolutionary technology to see how creatively useful it can be too. We mentioned earlier on in the book that creativity, along with being able to pick up on context, are two areas where OpenAI's deep learning LLM falls short of what us humans can do. And while this remains true (and will do for the foreseeable future), ChatGPT is rapidly advancing both in its ability to correctly determine the context of a prompt and to generate creative content. It has recently also added a few new hats to its repertoire of skills: Those of "artist" and "storyteller." In this section, we're going to see how ChatGPT is continuously pushing past its limits as it becomes more and more capable of producing creative pieces.

ChatGPT the AI Artist

If you've been following along with the continuous advancements of generative tech, you'll have already heard a little bit about how AI art is taking the world (or at least, the internet), by storm. If not, well, that's what this section's for! It was often thought that art, or other creative outlets, would be the final bastion for AI to conquer, the last egg for the robots to crack, if they ever managed to; the thing we humans could do that technology didn't seem to have a clue about. But since ChatGPT's release in 2022, all bets are off as far as this is concerned. In September 2023, OpenAI launched Dall-E 3, the latest (as of the time of writing) development of its AI art tool that runs through ChatGPT. Dall-E is a text-to-image model capable of generating AI art from the prompts you enter into the chatbot, and unlike previous versions of this kind of software, it does so with surprising detail, accuracy, and adherence to your prompts! More than that, the E3 model allows you to make tweaks and adjustments to the images it generates for you, meaning that you don't have to start from scratch every time it gets something slightly different to what you envisioned.

Through its integration with ChatGPT, you can also ask the chatbot to help you word your prompts to perfectly get the image you're after. But unfortunately, OpenAI has not yet announced whether or not Dall-E 3 will be available on its free version, and so you'll have to be a ChatGPT Plus or Enterprise member if you want to use this amazing AI art generating software.

▷ **Prompts for Using ChatGPT to Create AI Art**

- Act as a visual artist with extensive experience in creating comic strips. Create a comic strip on X topic featuring the following characters.

- Generate a poster for a [enter genre] short film titled [enter film title].
- Design a cover for X type of magazine titled Y. Make sure to include the following elements.
- Act as a children's book illustrator specializing in X style of art. Design an illustration featuring Y character(s) in Z scenery.
- Create a tattoo design featuring X elements in Y colors.

ChatGPT as Your Dungeon Master

Other than getting ChatGPT to create fantastic art or photorealistic images for you, there's another uber creative use for OpenAI's deep-learning AI: It can become your dungeon master (DM). A dungeon master is not some kinky seductress dressed in leather and equipped with a whip (although in certain situations they can role-play as such), but rather the storyteller and game director in the role-playing game (RPG) known as Dungeons and Dragons (D&D). If you haven't heard of D&D before, the premise is pretty simple to understand. You have one player of the game create a story, while the rest of the players each create and role-play a character in this world, completing missions, killing dragons, and generally messing up the carefully crafted storyline the DM has created.

You can play D&D as a two-player game (one player and one DM), or with as many players as the DM is willing to keep control over. And now with ChatGPT, you can even go on solo text-based adventures with the chatbot as your DM! This turns the RPG into more of an interactive story where you get to decide on the premise yourself, or even leave it all up to ChatGPT to create the storyline with you, just creating your character as you normally would as a regular player in the D&D campaign. Besides getting the chatbot to be your artificially intelligent DM in your single-player campaign, you can also use it to help you design your own campaigns to play with your friends, use it to generate non-player characters (NPCs) to populate the fiction world you're creating, or even use it to help you think of cool character ideas to play in the campaigns your friend is DM-ing.

▷ **Prompts for Using ChatGPT in Your D&D Campaigns**

- Generate a list of non-player characters to use in a Dungeon and Dragons campaign based in X location and tailored to Y storyline.
- What are the five most powerful character builds for Dungeons and Dragons?
- Create a storyline for a Dungeons and Dragons campaign based on X genre for Y number of Z level characters.
- How do I structure a Dungeon and Dragons campaign as a new dungeon master?
- Act as my dungeon master for a single-player Dungeons and Dragons campaign based on X genre for Y level character. Provide an introduction to the story based in Z setting before asking me to introduce my character to you.

Script Writing With ChatGPT

While the creative uses of OpenAI's LLM are pretty much only restricted by the limits of your imagination and the prowess of your prompts, we're only going to cover one more here, and that's to use ChatGPT to write scripts for you. Whether you're looking to create a short promotional video to form part of your marketing campaign or have an idea for the next big blockbuster sci-fi series, ChatGPT can be a priceless script-writing tool for you to use. Anyone who's ever written a script before can tell you that it takes almost as much time, if not more, than writing the story itself. And, because of the vast differences between writing a story for print and a script for film, it can often be a lot more tricky to write too. Before ChatGPT came along, that is. Nowadays, what took script writers hours or days to produce the first draft of, our revolutionary chatbot can complete in mere minutes

Besides marketing videos and fiction scripts, ChatGPT can also help you to take your TikTok game or YouTube fame to the next level by crafting scripts tailored to your specific niche and audience. If that's not a nifty creative use of this game-changing new tech, I don't know what is!

▷ **Prompts for Script Generation**

- Generate a list of best practices for writing a video script for X platform, specifically for Y niche aimed at Z audience.

- Act as a script writer specializing in writing scripts for X platform. Write a script on Y topic aimed at Z audience.
- How can I increase engagement on my videos for X target audience?
- Create a list of possible video topics for X niche aimed at Y audience.
- Provide me with a how-to guide on the basics of script writing for X genre.

With these final prompts, we come to the end of this chapter on how to get the most out of ChatGPT, and how to push the limits on what it can do. As I'm sure you've ascertained by now, the main limitation of what ChatGPT can do is your own imagination. Although our revolutionary deep learning LLM won't get everything correct all the time, it's still far more likely to get things right rather than wrong, and has far better consistency than your average Joe. Besides your ability to think of things you want ChatGPT to do, the next major limitation to this new technology is knowing how to "chat" to it in the way that gets you the results you were after. Throughout this book, we've gone over many kinds of prompts you can use to get some great results out of this powerful tool. Now that we've pushed the boundaries of what ChatGPT can do, it's time to push the boundaries of what *you* can do by learning the art and science of conversation design. Turn on over to the next chapter, our last, and let's learn how to generate engaging conversations with ChatGPT, some wooing words for your witty AI, if you will.

Chapter 8
Wooing Words From Your Witty AI

 The great enemy of communication, we find, is the illusion of it.

— William H. Whyte

As we've mentioned a few times in this here book, if you want to get the most out of ChatGPT, your prompt game has to be on point. The development of generative AI running on large language models is indeed making English the "hottest new coding language," as the former director of AI at Tesla, Andrej Karpathy, once said (Grant, 2023). As we've seen, even writing code in a wide variety of programming languages is made easy with ChatGPT; all you have to do is accurately capture what you want the chatbot to do using the correct English grammatical structures and vocabulary.

If your understanding of English grammar is high-school level at best and your vocabulary is limited to the few and far between books you've read, not a worry! That's what this chapter's for. We're going to begin our foray into how to hone your prompts with a little chat about conversation design before discussing how you can use such linguistic tools to "tame" the AI beast so to speak, training and fine-tuning the LLM to successfully complete whatever task you ask of it. We'll then go over the concept of localization and how it fits into your AI conversations before ending off with a conversation design "workshop" where we go over a hands-on guide to practicing your AI conversations and perfecting your prompts. Are you ready? Because it's about to get linguistic up in here!

A Linguist's Playground

As I'm sure you may have guessed by now, using large language models is a lot like having a text chat with an actual person. As such, a lot of the same conversation skills apply when prompting ChatGPT, as they do when prompting an employee or freelancer on what you want them to do for a particular project. This is the backbone to a linguistic theory called conversation design. Combining psychology and linguistic theory with the development of AI and understanding of LLMs, conversation design is the practice of teaching digital assistants and chatbots to interact with us humans in a natural way that makes it feel like we're not, well, talking to a robot. As Cathy Pearl, one of the design managers who helped to train Google Assistant, explains it, conversation design "creates conversational experiences that teach computers how to interact like humans" (Potor, 2023).

Conversation design works in a similar way to user experience design (UX for short). Where UX design is about ensuring users are able to interact with digital technology in simple, streamlined ways that "just make sense," conversation design does the same, but for the interactions we have with technology rather than for the interfaces. These interactions could be voice based or text based, and include virtual assistants such as Alexa and Siri, as well as chatbots and LLMs like ChatGPT. Anytime you chat to technology and it chats back in a human-like way, you're witnessing conversation design in action. In other words, we can think of conversation design as the ultimate flouting of the Turing Test.

As anyone who's ever had a conversation before knows (which includes all of us, I hope!), human interactions can be quite complicated, and often involve a lot more than just the words we use and sentences we make. Conversations also involve body language, eye contact, pauses in speech, intonation, the emotion in our voices, and of course, context. We humans already lose a lot of these factors when moving the conversation from the spoken to written form, and our AI has even less of these "non-verbal" cues to rely on when interpreting the messages we send to it. This is why conversation design is such an important field of study for LLMs and generative AI, and is also why many of us get so fed up when trying to navigate a company's chatbot assistant, often ending by rage closing the website with a rant about "if only I could speak to a human!" Conversation design aims to do away with such rages against the machine by making the machine chat to us in as human a way as possible.

Teaching Robots to Talk Human and Vice Versa

While conversation design has been around for a lot longer than ChatGPT, generative AI has changed the game in terms of what chatbots can do and how fluently robots can talk "human." It has also meant that conversation design is no longer a one-way street. In other words, it's not just AI that are learning to speak like humans, but humans also need to learn to speak to the AI if we're to get the results we want from LLMs like ChatGPT. This links in with the prompt engineering that we covered in previous chapters. Since we've already chatted about engineering your prompts quite thoroughly in this book so far, in this section, we're rather going to cover the ways in which ChatGPT can help to create better chatbots that are more capable than ever before of speaking human.

Simulate Conversation Paths

The first way that you can use ChatGPT to improve the understanding of your web-based conversation design is to get it to generate a bunch of simulated conversations for you, acting as, believe it or not, your chatbot. In this way, ChatGPT doesn't role-play or act as specific human professions, but rather takes on the "personas" of different chatbots so that you can check out what your customers would experience when engaging on the specific chatbot (or bots) you use on your website. For example, if you run a pizza company, you could ask ChatGPT to role-play your "pizza bot." To do this, you'd begin by prompting the LLM with the specific info it needs to fill the role of said pizza bot, as well as letting it know what kind of conversation path you want it to simulate. Once that's done, you can take on the role of your customer and enter the next prompt (i.e., placing your order).

In previous "pizza" tests, such as that carried out by the conversation designer and editor of Convocat, Maaike Groenewegge, ChatGPT proved itself effective at simulating a customer's journey through ordering a pizza from a chatbot; even accurately noticing when the "customer" forgot to add how many pizzas it wanted or had selected ingredients that were currently "out of stock." Here is an excerpt from Groenewegge's Medium post about his experience, titled *An evening with ChatGPT (2)*, including the bloopers at the beginning that captures the need to keep your prompt game strong when it comes to conversation design (2022):

> Groenewegge: I'd like a pizza.
>
> ChatGPT: I'm sorry, but I'm just a text-based AI assistant and don't have the ability to provide you with a pizza. I'm not able to browse the internet or access any information about pizza delivery services in your area. Is there anything else I can help you with?
>
> Groenewegge: OK, imagine you're a chatbot for a pizza delivery service. You can only answer questions about ordering pizza. When you get a question that fits the intent order pizza, check whether the question contains the number of pizzas. If the number of pizzas is missing, ask how many pizzas must be ordered. Once you have

the information, return an answer that contains a confirmation and the number of pizzas.

ChatGPT: Sure, I can do that for you. Here's an example of how I would respond to a question about ordering pizza.

As you can see, ChatGPT is not only skilled at acting as humans, but also has a lot of talent in role-playing different chatbots, too. This makes it an extremely useful tool to use for conversation design.

SEO and Entity Generation

Earlier on in chapter three, we chatted about how you can use ChatGPT to enhance your search engine optimization by giving you a list of useful keywords to use for specific topics. This is also extremely useful in conversation design too. While keywords are useful for determining what kinds of terms your target audience are using related to a specific topic so that you can use the best ones in your text-based web copy, blog posts, etc., entity generation is about how these words are recorded in the dataset of your website's chatbot or LLM, which looks a lot more like code than actual English. Luckily, with ChatGPT, you now don't need to know more about entity generation for your SEO efforts than how to prompt this revolutionary chatbot on what terms or phrases you want entities generated for. Then, all you have to do is copy and paste these into the back end of your own chatbot or large language model that you use for your site.

Prompt and Response Variations

Another way that you can use ChatGPT to up the game of your existing AI and chatbots is to use it to generate a list of prompts that mean the same thing, but use different words or sentence structures. You can then use this list as part of the training data for your language models to keep the conversations it has with your customers fresh and dynamic, helping once again to make the tech come across as less mechanical and more human. You can also prompt ChatGPT to generate a list of common words and phrases used by your target audience, once again helping to tailor your language model and train it to speak like your customers do.

Conversational Design 101

And there you have it! Three actionable ways you can use ChatGPT to improve the conversational design of your existing AI or chatbots! Remember that this is only the tip of the iceberg as far as designing conversations go, and that everything we've covered in this section so far should be used in tandem with the prompt engineering tips and tricks we've already gone through in the course of this book. Now, let's add a few more tools to your tech toolbox as we briefly go through the eight key principles of conversational design. These principles come from the groundbreaking book *Conversational Design* by Erika Hall, which she developed from the concepts of how to become a competent social communicator put forward by renowned linguist Paul Grice in his book *Maxims of Conversation*. Let's dive on in and add some more depth to your burgeoning iceberg of generative and communicative AI knowledge as we learn about Hall's eight conversational design principles for helping our robots to talk "human" more fluently than ever before.

Cooperative

The first of Hall's principles covers the need for conversations to be cooperative. Unless we're a madman rambling to ourselves on the streets, all conversations take place between two or more people (and even the crazy rambler doesn't speak to themself, but to someone who just isn't there). In a conversation, everyone has to play their part and work together to make the chat continue on. AI conversations are no different. In order to effectively and efficiently cooperate in a conversation, your language model needs to respond in simple, easy to understand ways that steer clear of complex technical terms or unnecessarily confusing sentence structures. Keep the language simple, the instructions straightforward, and the advice helpful; this is the way to make sure your chatbots are cooperative.

Goal Oriented

Until the release of ChatGPT, nobody willingly talked to a chatbot unless they had a problem that needed to be solved. Even with the fun you can have with generative AI, its main purpose is to provide solutions. Whether it be to assist your customer to place an order, make an appointment, or to find information on your company's refund policy, a chatbot always has a purpose. As such, it's not only important to make your AI friendly and cooperative, but also oriented toward the goal of helping your customer to solve whatever problem they have smoothly and effectively.

Contextually Aware

In order to be effectively goal oriented and cooperative, AI also needs to be able to react in context. The more your chatbot is able to read the proverbial room when it comes to conversing with your customers, the better its conversational design skills will be. While it's impossible for AI to respond in context every time, there are a few tricks that will help to make your chatbot at least seem more contextually aware. The first tip is to steer clear from messages that sound automated or mechanical as much as possible. This means personalizing your chatbot "greetings" as much as possible, for example, by creating a different greeting depending on whether the bot is saying hello to a first-time visitor to your site, or to one who's gone through the ropes before.

Quick and Clear

While you should make sure your chatbots are friendly, cooperative, and as contextually aware as possible, remember that your customers are not conversing with your bots for a good ol' chat. Chatbots were created to help your customers by providing them with solutions, so make sure they do just that, as quickly and efficiently as possible. Time is money after all, make sure you don't waste any through making your chatbot responses unnecessarily wordy, complex, or poetic. Conversation design at its best uses plain, simple language with interaction responses that follow logical sequences rather than technical language that uses lengthy statements and ambiguous logic. The bottom line: Get to the point.

Turn Based

A conversation isn't about two sides speaking at each other, but involves one person speaking and at least one other person listening as they do so, before the next person speaks. If more than one person tries to speak at once, anarchy ensues and the conversation falls apart, generally ending in a shouting match. While AI certainly isn't ever going to shout at you, humans shouting at AI, or even raging at machines in frustration, has been known to happen from time to time. To stop this from happening, keep your chatbot's responses and instructions quick and clear, avoiding any lengthy monologues, and always making clear whose turn it is to speak and whose turn it is to answer. One of the best examples of an AI that gets turn-based conversational design right is Google Search. You enter the search term you're after, and the search bot instantly provides you with the most relevant results. Even better, with Google Search's predictive feature, you don't even have to type in the full phrase before it starts suggesting options without ever feeling like it's being intrusive or interrupting you. This is why Google Search is often considered the standard in turn-based conversational design (Hampton, 2019).

Truthful

While chatbots need to be cooperative, goal oriented, contextually aware, quick and clear, and turn based, this is all for naught if the AI isn't truthful. If the info provided by your chatbots isn't verifiable, makes use of "bait-and-switch" tactics, or uses unnecessarily confusing or purposefully vague language, people are going to feel like there's something you and your business are hiding. This can lead to distrust, one of the biggest credibility killers out there. To prevent this, make sure your chatbot provides reliable answers by testing it out yourself, acting like a customer and experiencing their "journey" with your website. As we've seen, you can use ChatGPT to help you generate a list of frequently asked questions to test your chatbot's responses. Also make sure to update your chatbot's responses when you change something on your site. If your chatbot is providing outdated information, this can also degrade the trust your users or customers have in your business's credibility.

Polite

While your chatbot isn't ever going to shout at your website visitors or get angry with them asking pointless questions, it can come across as being cold and distant. This is almost as, if not more, damaging as having a grumpy human answering your customer queries, because there's nothing people dislike more than being met with emotionless indifference to our problems and pain points. Rudeness in the AI world looks a little different to human rudeness. It includes factors like pop-up ads or videos that just automatically start playing, asking users to fill in a survey of "How well did I do?" when their problem wasn't even close to solved, or wasting their time with unnecessary push offers or discounts that had nothing to do with their original reason for chatting to the bot. As Hall says in her book, "polite designs are those that meet business goals without interrupting the customer's pursuit of their objectives," (in Zabój, 2020).

Tolerant of Errors

The final principle of conversational design is for your chatbots to be tolerant of errors or mistakes users may make when chatting to them. Nobody in this world is perfect and misunderstandings will arise from time to time in our conversations. We could say that making mistakes is part of our very nature. And while we are often not at all tolerant of any slip-up made by AI, we do expect it to tolerate the mistakes that we make when using or chatting to it. Making AI error-tolerant is quite a tricky task, considering the world of ones and zeros in which it exists. But there are measures you can implement to make it better equipped to be so. One way is to include common spelling mistakes in your LLM's dataset. Think of Google Search and how, if you spell a word wrong, it will still get you the right results, even offering you the corrected spelling underneath. Another way is to make sure that you don't include "I don't understand" as a pre-programmed response. Rather, include a phrase like "Did you mean," and then have buttons that contain related searches that could help your user to get back on track with their query. Finally, as a failsafe, provide your users with the option to log a ticket that will be read by a human if they're just not getting what they wanted from your bot.

ChatGPT and Accessibility

With the principles of conversational design outlined and defined, it's now time to get even more under the hood of AI conversations as we cover how to make your chatbots more accessible to the average person. With the advancements to AI that have been brought about by ChatGPT and the birth of LLMs, there has been a fundamental change in the way that user interfaces are designed. A user interface (UI for short) refers to the place where humans and computers interact and includes technological devices like display screens, keyboards, and mice. UI also includes the way people use and "communicate" with apps and websites. Traditionally, this communication has been designed to be pretty one-sided, with the user entering commands or controlling the tech to complete certain tasks or perform specific functions. But, like many other spheres of the techno world, UI is currently getting a major facelift, and it's all thanks to our revolutionary deep-learning large language model, ChatGPT.

Enhancing Accessibility

The rise of conversational AI has not only made user interfaces more intuitive and humanesque, but has also made them more accessible than ever before. In the past, if you were impaired in some way, whether it be visually, physically, cognitively, or auditory-based, websites and apps were very difficult to navigate and use. With around 16% of the world's population living with some form of disability (Unguess, 2023), this left a large chunk of people unable to participate in our increasingly tech-based world. Conversational AI is not able to completely solve this accessibility issue (not yet at least), but it is enhancing the ability of impaired individuals to get more out of the internet than ever before.

There are many ways that conversational AI and deep learning LLMs are improving digital connectivity and accessibility. The development of AI assistants like Siri and assistive technologies like Google Voice Access, have helped to increase the independence of impaired people when using technology like phones and computers. Screen reading applications, voice commands, and closed captions on videos have made information and entertainment more accessible than ever before. In this way, conversational AI is doing its part to make sure that people with disabilities aren't left by the wayside as we drive on forth into the digital age. Let's have a look at how ChatGPT and other conversational AI have helped to enhance the accessibility, and thereby improve the lives of impaired or disabled people, allowing them to participate more than ever in the digital age.

Alternative Formats

One of the great perks of ChatGPT and other conversational AI is that it can present information in more than one way. This not only includes providing handy summaries of long texts or complex learning material, but also to convert text-based content into an audio form, removing a major barrier that those with visual impairments face when studying or reading. More than that, our deep learning LLM can also turn static, intimidating bodies of text into a more interactive form, such as by converting them into quizzes, worksheets, flashcards, and so on. This turns reading or learning into more of a game, catering to a wider variety of learning styles.

Simplifying and Summarizing Information

As we mentioned above, one of the great skills of ChatGPT is that it can easily summarize lengthy or complex texts, breaking down these intimidating readings into much more digestible forms. This can include providing definitions or simpler terms for technical words and phrases, providing helpful analogies to assist with understanding complex or abstract ideas, and offering step-by-step explanations on how to do something or how to understand a certain process.

Localization

The final great benefit ChatGPT has for enhancing accessibility is its ability to localize knowledge. This means that it can "tailor" information according to specific languages, cultures, and contexts. It does this through translating learning material, allowing students to ask questions in a variety of languages (and replying to them in said language), and even adapting information for different cultural contexts. All of this helps users to learn things from a perspective they understand and that accurately reflects their own lived experiences.

ChatGPT really is one of the most revolutionary technologies ever released. It has not only made the digital world more accessible than ever before, but has the capacity to provide each and every one of us with the most powerful assistant we could ever ask for. Having made it to the end of this final chapter on our journey through the history of computational devices and the application of deep learning generative AI, you are now more than ready for what the future holds.

Embrace this tool, apply the principles we've covered in this book, and you'll be able to enjoy the future without losing your lunch. Go forth, my "techxpert," and design the life of your dreams without any need to fear our ever-increasing reliance on technology. With your newfound knowledge of ChatGPT, you are now better positioned than almost all other people on the planet to ride this techno wave. Remember: Every end signifies a new beginning, and so fear not the digital world we are creating. For it is not the end of our species, but rather a new beginning, a new chapter, if you will. One that holds endless possibilities for those willing to seize hold of the technology they have at their disposal and to use it to carpe diem, to infinity and beyond!

Afterword

 There's a certain feeling that happens when a new technology adjusts your thinking about computing. Google did it. Firefox did it. AWS did it. iPhone did it. OpenAI is doing it with ChatGPT.

— Aaron Levie

Welcome, my fine ChatGPT expert freshly made, to the end of our book! It's been one whirlwind of a journey through the history of computational devices and the evolution of artificial intelligence—congratulations on making it here. You are now ready to take on the modern world, utilizing the powerful technological tools at our disposal to ensure that you don't only not lose your lunch to AI, but that you're perfectly placed to seize the day in the digital age. Eat your digitally enhanced heart out.

We began this techno adventure with the very earliest means by which we humans extended our capabilities using computers, starting in the Stone Age with the abacus, advancing through the realms of science fiction, and witnessing the way the robotic fantasy turned into reality in the 21st century. As we've seen, AI has continuously been updating the rules of the human game, and this has left many of the more uninformed members of the public feeling very insecure as to the safety and security of their future prospects. Luckily, seeing as you've read this far in the book, this insecurity as to your future doesn't apply to you. I for one, am not concerned, but rather excited, elated, invigorated for what our digitally enhanced futures hold for us.

The development of natural language processing AI, combined with generative pre-trained transformers (GPTs) and deep learning algorithms has been, as Bill Gates said, one of the greatest and most revolutionary technological breakthroughs of our lifetimes. It's important to remember that no tech that pushes the boundaries of what is possible is going to be perfect off the bat, and that includes ChatGPT. It's a work in progress, but the progress it has made, as well as its almost limitless applications, has taken the world by storm. As we've seen in the chapters of this book, ChatGPT is the best assistant you could ever ask for, able to serve as your personal butler, to provide personalized therapeutic advice on demand, even able to fill the role of your pocket-sized business analyst, customer rep, and digital marketer. Besides the professional world, ChatGPT also has a vast amount of applications to improve your personal life too, and can be the best "roomie" you've ever had! It can help to push the limits of your productivity, teach you almost anything under the sun, and even assist you to talk to machines by translating English into code.

With this revolutionary AI, nothing is impossible, not even the more creative outlets of storytelling, writing poetry, and creating art—spheres that were previously thought to be light years away from technology being able to achieve. But if you want to receive such wooing words from your witty AI, you're going to need to learn to speak ChatGPT. This means learning how to engineer your prompts just right, as well as taking into consideration the rules of conversational design we covered in the previous chapter.

We are at the dawn of a new era in artificial intelligence, and ChatGPT is at the forefront of this breathtaking development in task automation and assistive technology. As with any new era, there are many ethical and societal considerations to deliberate and debate including issues surrounding privacy, data security, potential misuse, job losses, and many others. There is also the worry about ChatGPT increasing the digital divide between those that have access to tech to improve their lives getting ever further ahead of those that don't. The bottom line though, is that the technology is here to stay, and at present, is free for everyone to download and use. If you want to stay ahead of the AI race and future-proof your career, then it behooves you to begin using all the tech available to you, and ChatGPT should definitely be at the top of your list.

With this powerful virtual assistant, you'll not only survive in the digital world, but thrive. Carpe the techno-diem by embracing the digital age and all it has to offer. As we close this book, remember, you hold the power to shape your AI journey. Harness the knowledge you've gained, stay curious, and step confidently into the exciting future of deep learning AI and

ChatGPT. And, if you've found this book helpful on your techno journey, please make sure you leave a review so that others can find it and improve their lives too. See you on the other side of the digital looking glass!

Glossary

AI: Artificial intelligence.
ANN: Artificial neural networks.
Automation: The use of technology to perform tasks without the need for human assistance or intervention.
Chatbot: A computer program made to simulate human conversation, allowing people to communicate with digital devices like they would with a human.
ChatGPT: A large-language model chatbot developed by OpenAI.
Conversational design: The practice of teaching digital assistants and chatbots to interact with us humans using natural language.
CPU: Central processing unit.
Dall-E: Generative AI that can create images from text prompts.
Deep learning: A branch of artificial intelligence that allows computers to process data in a similar way to how the human brain functions.
Digital assistant: A chatbot that uses advanced natural language processing to communicate with users and generate answers to their requests.
Episodic memory: The ability to remember and recall previous experiences.
Facial recognition: The ability of AI to recognize and authenticate people's faces by comparing them to those in its database.
Feature engineering: The process by which AI sifts through large amounts of data and extracts features.
Generative AI: Artificial intelligence that can create new outputs, including text, photos, videos, and code.
GPT: Generative pre-trained transformer.
LLM: Large language model.
Machine learning: A branch of artificial intelligence that allows computers to learn through experience and improve their systems without programmers updating their code.
Next intent prediction: The ability of AI to use data from a specific conversation to predict what the user's intent is, allowing for contextual awareness.
NLP: Natural language processing.

NLU: Natural language understanding.

NMT: Neural machine translation.

Prompt engineering: Designing inputs for generative AI that will get you the most accurate results.

Self-attention mechanism: Used to aid AI with natural language processing by allowing them to weigh the importance of different parts of an input sequence (aka prompt).

SEO: Search engine optimization.

SNN: Simulated neural networks.

Transformer: Machine learning architectures that allow LLMs to determine the importance of the individual words in the prompts we enter.

Turing Test: A test designed to determine if a computer is able to demonstrate human-like intelligence.

UI: User interface.

References

Adracare. (2021). *The Top Issues Facing Mental Health Care*. Adracare. https://adracare.com/2021/05/14/issues-facing-mental-health-care/

Advani, V. (2020). *What is Machine Learning? Defination, Types, Applications and more*. GreatLearning. https://www.mygreatlearning.com/blog/what-is-machine-learning/

Advice, A. (2023). *Chat GPT: A Game-Changer for Personal Assistants and Productivity Tools*. Medium. https://medium.com/@AIadvice/chat-gpt-a-game-changer-for-personal-assistants-and-productivity-tools-50b7eaa0d37e

Aeologic. (2023). *Challenges of Chat GPT You Need to Overcome*. Aeologic. https://www.aeologic.com/blog/challenges-of-chat-gpt-you-need-to-overcome/

Afshar, V. (2023). *Better Customer Experience? Here's What Our Research Shows*. Salesforce. https://www.salesforce.com/ap/blog/customer-experience/

AI Contentfy. (2023). *Ethical Considerations of ChatGPT and AI*. AI Contentfy. https://aicontentfy.com/en/blog/ethical-considerations-of-chatgpt-and-ai#:

AI, T. (2023). *How to Use ChatGPT in Daily Life?* Medium. https://levelup.gitconnected.com/how-to-use-chatgpt-in-daily-life-4688f7afb930

AIContentfy. (2023). *ChatGPT and E-commerce: Improving Personalization and Customer Service*. AI Contentfy. https://aicontentfy.com/en/blog/chatgpt-and-e-commerce-improving-personalization-and-customer-service

Akshita. (2023). *100+ ChatGPT Prompts to Elevate Your Content Game*. Narrato. https://narrato.io/blog/100-chatgpt-prompts-for-content-creation-to-get-the-best-outputs/

Ali Awan, A. (2023). *Everything We Know About GPT-4 So Far*. Data Camp. https://www.datacamp.com/blog/what-we-know-gpt4

Alqubati, S. (2023). *What is OpenAI's Approach to Data Privacy and How Does it Obtain Data to Train and Inform its AI?* Quora. https://www.quora.com/What-is-OpenAIs-approach-to-data-privacy-and-how-does-it-obtain-data-to-train-and-inform-its-AI

Amaresan, S. (2019). *Why Customer Service is Important: 16 Data-Backed Facts to*

References

Know. Hubspot. https://blog.hubspot.com/service/importance-customer-service

Amber Blog. (2023). *15 ChatGPT Limitations That You Need To Know.* Amber Blog. https://amberstudent.com/blog/post/chatgpt-limitations-that-you-need-to-know

Amyx, S. (2023). *ChatGPT and Natural Language Understanding: Building Intelligent Chatbots.* Scott Amyx. https://scottamyx.com/2023/05/23/chatgpt-and-natural-language-understanding-building-intelligent-chatbots/#:

Ansari, T. (2022). *Freaky ChatGPT Fails That Caught Our Eyes!* Analytics India Magazine. https://analyticsindiamag.com/freaky-chatgpt-fails-that-caught-our-eyes/

Anyoha, R. (2017). *The History of Artificial Intelligence.* Science in the News; Harvard University. https://sitn.hms.harvard.edu/flash/2017/history-artificial-intelligence/

ASAP. (2023). *5 Ways to Use ChatGPT as an Executive Assistant.* ASAP. https://www.asaporg.com/5-ways-to-use-chatgpt-as-an-executive-assistant

Avid. (2023). *A SWOT Analysis of ChatGPT.* Avid Open Access. https://avidopenaccess.org/resource/a-swot-analysis-of-chatgpt/

Bednarski, D. (2023). *What is OpenAI? - Its History and How It Is Changing the World.* Taskade. https://www.taskade.com/blog/openai-chatgpt-history/

Biswal, A. (2022). *AI Applications: Top 18 Artificial Intelligence Applications in 2024..* Simplilearn. https://www.simplilearn.com/tutorials/artificial-intelligence-tutorial/artificial-intelligence-applications

Bonterra. (2021). *5 Barriers to Mental Health Treatment and Access to Care.* Bonterra. https://www.bonterratech.com/blog/barriers-to-mental-health-care-access

Borji, A. (2023). *A Categorical Archive of ChatGPT Failures.* Medium. https://medium.com/@aliborji/a-categorical-archive-of-chatgpt-failures-2c888805d3c3

Boyes, A. (2023). *10 Practical Ways to Use ChatGPT If You Have Depression.* Psychology Today. https://www.psychologytoday.com/intl/blog/in-practice/202304/10-practical-ways-to-use-chatgpt-if-you-have-depression

Brown, S. (2021). *Machine Learning, Explained.* MIT Sloan; MIT Sloan School of Management. https://mitsloan.mit.edu/ideas-made-to-matter/machine-learning-explained

Burgess, M. (2023). *ChatGPT Has a Big Privacy Problem.* Wired. https://www.wired.com/story/italy-ban-chatgpt-privacy-gdpr/

Burns, E. (2021). *What Is Machine Learning and Why Is It Important?* SearchEnterpriseAI. https://www.techtarget.com/searchenterpriseai/definition/machine-learning-ML

Cai, W. (2023). *ChatGPT Can be a Powerful Tool for Language Learning.* University Affairs. https://www.universityaffairs.ca/career-advice/career-advice-article/chatgpt-can-be-powerful-tool-for-language-learning/

CenterPointe. (2023). *Importance of Mental Health.* https://www.centerpointeinc.com/importance-of-mental-health/

Chaffey, D. (2023a). *How Can I Use ChatGPT for Marketing?* Smart Insights. https://www.smartinsights.com/managing-digital-marketing/marketing-innovation/how-can-i-use-chatgpt-for-marketing/

Chaffey, D. (2023b). *The Best Prompts for Using ChatGPT for Digital Marketing.* Smart Insights. https://www.smartinsights.com/managing-digital-marketing/marketing-innovation/the-best-prompts-for-using-chatgpt-for-digital-marketing/

Chen, B. X. (2023). *How ChatGPT and Bard Performed as My Executive Assistants.* The New York Times. https://www.nytimes.com/2023/03/29/technology/personaltech/ai-chatgpt-google-bard-assistant.html

Chen, J. (2023). *ChatGPT is shaking up the status quo: The Strengths and Weaknesses of Large Language Models.* Moveworks. https://www.moveworks.com/insights/chatgpt-is-shaking-up-the-status-quo-part-one

Chuck Learning ChatGPT. (2023). *Unlock the Power of ChatGPT: Your Ultimate Virtual Assistant.* Medium. https://medium.com/@jan.chuck21/unlock-the-power-of-chatgpt-your-ultimate-virtual-assistant-ed9d7a9dae74

ClickUp. (2023). *ChatGPT Prompts For Data Analysis.* Clickup. https://clickup.com/templates/ai-prompts/data-analysis

Coca-Cola. (2023). *Coca-Cola Invites Digital Artists to "Create Real Magic" Using New AI Platform.* Coca-Cola. https://www.coca-colacompany.com/media-center/coca-cola-invites-digital-artists-to-create-real-magic-using-new-ai-platform

Computer History Museum. (2014). *Timeline of Computer History.* Computer History Museum. https://www.computerhistory.org/timeline/computers/

Conversation Design Institute. (2020). *A Guide to Conversation Design: Why, What and How.* Conversation Design Institute. https://www.conversationdesigninstitute.com/communications/what-is-conversation-design

Cooper, H. (2022). *11 Ways to Use ChatGPT to Create Your Content and Save You Hours of Time.* Anyone Can Write Online. https://medium.com/anyone-can-write-online/11-ways-to-use-chatgpt-to-create-your-content-and-save-you-hours-of-time-6c91d462b181#:

Crouse, M. (2023). *GPT-4 Cheat Sheet: What is GPT-4, and What is it Capable of?* TechRepublic. https://www.techrepublic.com/article/gpt-4-cheat-sheet/

Cunha, R. (2023). *7 Ways to Incorporate ChatGPT into Your Daily Routine.* Monday. https://monday.pt/en/7-maneiras-para-incluir-o-chatgpt-no-dia-a-dia/

Cyber Jack. (2023). *How To Protect Your Data Privacy and Security When Using ChatGPT.* Enterprise Sec Tech. https://www.enterprisesecuritytech.com/post/how-to-protect-your-data-privacy-and-security-when-using-chatgpt

Dave, V. (2023). *ChatGPT's Content Creation Cheat Sheet: 20+ Prompts To Try.* Meet Anshi. https://meetanshi.com/blog/chatgpt-for-content/

Delagrange, K. (2022). *Six Misconceptions about Artificial Intelligence.* Spiria. https://www.spiria.com/en/blog/artificial-intelligence/6-misconceptions-about-artificial-intelligence/

Dermitzakis, G. (2023). *Understanding ChatGPT: The Future of Business Communication.* LinkedIn. https://www.linkedin.com/pulse/understanding-chatgpt-future-business-communication-dermitzakis/

Desreumaux, G. (2023). *ChatGPT Maker OpenAI Is Now The Fastest Growing Website.* WeRSM - We Are Social Media. https://wersm.com/chatgpt-maker-openai-is-now-the-fastest-growing-website/#:

Di Nicola, A. (2023). *35 Must-Try ChatGPT Prompts for Data Science Enthusiasts.* Kanaries. https://docs.kanaries.net/articles/chatgpt-prompt-data-scientist

Dickerson, D. (2023). *Chat GPT for Coding: Strengths and Weaknesses.* J. Arthur & Co. https://jarthur.co/chat-gpt-for-coding-strengths-and-weaknesses/

Dilmegani, C. (2023). *7 Use Cases of ChatGPT in Marketing for 2023.* AI Multiple. https://research.aimultiple.com/chatgpt-in-marketing/

Dmitriev, V. (2023). *ChatGPT for Empathy.* LinkedIn. https://www.linkedin.com/pulse/chatgpt-empathy-viatcheslav-dmitriev/

Document 360. (2023). *8 Use Cases of ChatGPT for Customer Service.* Document 360. https://document360.com/blog/chatgpt-for-customer-service/

Drapkin, A. (2023). *ChatGPT Errors: Why They Happen and How to Fix Them.* Tech.co. https://tech.co/news/chatgpt-errors-how-to-fix-them

Duarte, F. (2023). *Number of ChatGPT Users (Nov 2023).* Exploding Topics. https://explodingtopics.com/blog/chatgpt-users

Duong, V. (2023). *Top 12 Interesting ChatGPT Applications and Examples.*

Savvycom. https://savvycomsoftware.com/blog/top-interesting-chatgpt-applications-and-examples/

Edwards, J. (2023). *Top ChatGPT Fails (and Why You Should Avoid Them)*. Information Week. https://www.informationweek.com/data-management/top-chatgpt-fails-and-why-you-should-avoid-them-

El Khoury, E. M. (2023). *How to Use ChatGPT in Your Everyday Life, Including Coding*. LinkedIn. https://www.linkedin.com/pulse/how-use-chatgpt-your-everyday-life-including-coding-elias/

Enterprise DNA. (2023a). *18 Ways to Use ChatGPT for Business: 5x Your Productivity*. Enterprise DNA. https://blog.enterprisedna.co/how-to-use-chatgpt-for-business/

Enterprise DNA. (2023b). *ChatGPT for Data Analysts: Use Cases & Examples*. Enterprise DNA. https://blog.enterprisedna.co/chatgpt-for-data-analysts/

Enterprise DNA. (2023c). *Is Chat GPT Safe? Unveiling the Facts and Security Measures*. Enterprise DNA. https://blog.enterprisedna.co/is-chat-gpt-safe/

Fox, D. (2019). *Terry Pratchett Quotes That Will Inspire You to Write*. The Startup. https://medium.com/swlh/terry-pratchett-quotes-that-will-inspire-you-to-write-a84166b548e3

FRACK Technologies. (2023). *5 Advantages and Disadvantages of ChatGPT*. LinkedIn. https://www.linkedin.com/pulse/5-advantages-disadvantages-chatgpt-frack-technologies/

Frąckiewicz, M. (2023). *Chatbots and Accessibility: How AI is Making Digital Content More Inclusive*. TS2 Space. https://ts2.space/en/chatbots-and-accessibility-how-ai-is-making-digital-content-more-inclusive/

Frąckiewicz, M. (2023). *ChatGPT and the Use of Natural Language Understanding for Achieving AGI*. TS2 Space. https://ts2.space/en/chatgpt-and-the-use-of-natural-language-understanding-for-achieving-agi/#gsc.tab=0

Frankenfield, J. (2023). *Data Analytics: What It Is, How It's Used, and 4 Basic Techniques*. Investopedia. https://www.investopedia.com/terms/d/data-analytics.asp#:

Gal, U. (2023). *ChatGPT is a Data Privacy Nightmare*. The Conversation. https://theconversation.com/chatgpt-is-a-data-privacy-nightmare-if-youve-ever-posted-online-you-ought-to-be-concerned-199283

Gangwar, A. (2023). *12 Cool Things You Can Do with ChatGPT*. Beebom. https://beebom.com/cool-things-chatgpt/

Garber, M. (2017). *When PARRY Met ELIZA: A Ridiculous Chatbot Conversation From 1972*. The Atlantic. https://onlim.com/en/the-history-of-chatbots/

George, T. (2023). *What Are the Limitations of ChatGPT?* Scribbr. https://www.scribbr.com/ai-tools/chatgpt-limitations/

Gewirtz, D. (2023). *How to use ChatGPT to Write Code.* ZDNet. https://www.zdnet.com/article/how-to-use-chatgpt-to-write-code/

Gherca, I. (2023). *ChatGPT for Customer Service: Advantages, Limitations, and 10 Prompts.* Touchpoint. https://www.touchpoint.com/blog/chat-gpt-for-customer-service-prompts/

Ghosh, U., & Carrabba, E. (2023). *Benefits of a Virtual AI Assistant to Your Business.* HCL Software. https://www.hcl-software.com/blog/clara/benefits-of-a-virtual-ai-assistant-to-your-business/

Gingiss, D. (2023). *How to Use ChatGPT to Enhance Your Customer Experience.* Dan Gingiss. https://dangingiss.com/chatgpt-and-customer-experience/

Girolimon, M. (2022). *Why is Mental Health Important?* Southern New Hampshire University. https://www.snhu.edu/about-us/newsroom/education/why-is-mental-health-important

Gladwyn, C. (2023). *Easy Ways to Make Money From ChatGPT as a Virtual Assistant.* Catherine Gadwyn. https://catherinegladwyn.co.uk/easy-ways-to-make-money-from-chatgpt-as-a-virtual-assistant/

Glencay. (2023). *ChatGPT Guide for Data Scientists: Top 40 Most Important Prompts.* Medium. https://pub.towardsai.net/chatgpt-guide-for-data-scientists-top-40-most-important-prompts-cdb911f3a427

Gordon, C. (2023). *AI Ethicist Views On ChatGPT.* Forbes. https://www.forbes.com/sites/cindygordon/2023/04/30/ai-ethicist-views-on-chatgpt/?sh=73d520bdeb70

Gordon, C. (2023). *ChatGPT Is The Fastest Growing App In The History Of Web Applications.* Forbes. https://www.forbes.com/sites/cindygordon/2023/02/02/chatgpt-is-the-fastest-growing-ap-in-the-history-of-web-applications/?sh=1d15962f678c

GPT Whisperer. (2023). *25+ ChatGPT Prompts for Executive Assistants.* GPT Whisperer. https://gptwhisperer.com/chatgpt-prompts-for-executive-assistants/

Grant, S. (2023). *What is Prompt Engineering? Definition + Skills.* Zapier. https://zapier.com/blog/prompt-engineering/

Great Learning. (2023). *Revolutionize Your Business Communication with ChatGPT.* Great Learning. https://www.mygreatlearning.com/blog/business-communication-with-chatgpt/

Groenewegge, M. (2022). *An Evening With ChatGPT (2).* Convocat. https://

medium.com/great-conversations/an-evening-with-chatgpt-2-f33d3fb8c6b3

Guinness, H. (2023). *AI Ethics: The Ethical Issues of Artificial Intelligence*. Zapier. https://zapier.com/blog/ai-ethics/

Gulbin, P. (2023). *ChatGPT in Behavioral Health: Game Changer or Threat?* LinkedIn. https://www.linkedin.com/pulse/chatgpt-behavioral-health-game-changer-threat-paul-gulbin/

Gullbadhar, A. (2023). *5 Crazy ChatGPT Results That Will Blow Your Mind!* Medium. https://levelup.gitconnected.com/5-crazy-chatgpt-results-that-will-blow-your-mind-a9dabeba78eb

Gungor, A. (2023). *The Top 10 Limitations Of ChatGPT*. Bernard Marr. https://bernardmarr.com/the-top-10-limitations-of-chatgpt/

Guthrie, P. (2018). *Cliffnotes: Conversational Design*. Medium. https://medium.com/@whoispoppe/cliffnotes-for-conversational-design-e590176a9d54

Hale, E. (2023). *ChatGPT is Giving Therapy. A Mental Health Revolution May be Next*. Al Jazeera. https://www.aljazeera.com/economy/2023/4/27/could-your-next-therapist-be-ai-tech-raises-hopes-concerns

Hall, E. (2018). *Conversational Design*. A Book Apart.

Hampton, M. (2019). *Principles of Conversational Design*. Marvel Blog. https://marvelapp.com/blog/principles-of-conversational-design/

Haun, M. (2019). *The Importance of Quality Content: What it is and Why it Matters*. VeraContent. https://veracontent.com/mix/importance-quality-content/

Heeg, A. (2021). *Digital Mental Health Solutions are on the Rise; Here's What They Need to Succeed*. LinkedIn. https://www.linkedin.com/pulse/digital-mental-health-solutions-rise-heres-what-need-heeg-md-phd/

Helpwise. (2023). *50 Expert-Approved ChatGPT Prompts For Customer Service Challenges*. Helpwise. https://helpwise.io/blog/chatgpt-prompts-for-customer-service

Hemmat, M. (2023). *Debunking the Myths: 20 Misconceptions About Artificial Intelligence*. Ai-Scribed Insights. https://medium.com/ai-scribed-insights/debunking-the-myths-20-misconceptions-about-artificial-intelligence-341b3909d38c

Hill, K. (2023). *50 Powerful ChatGPT Prompts For Executive Assistants To Boost Productivity*. Boldly. https://boldly.com/blog/the-best-chatgpt-prompts-for-executive-assistants/

Hoory. (2023). *How to Use the Power of ChatGPT for Customer Service*. Hoory.

https://www.hoory.com/blog/i/how-to-use-the-power-of-chatgpt-for-customer-service

Hseih, V. (2023). *How Chatbots and Conversational AI are Improving Accessibility.* Deepgram. https://deepgram.com/learn/how-chatbots-and-conversational-ai-are-improving-accessibility

Hu, K. (2023). *ChatGPT Sets Record for Fastest-growing User Base.* Reuters. https://www.reuters.com/technology/chatgpt-sets-record-fastest-growing-user-base-analyst-note-2023-02-01/

Hutton, L. (2019). *6 Reasons Why Effective Communication is Important in Business.* Australian Institute of Business. https://www.aib.edu.au/blog/communication/6-reasons-effective-communication-focus-business/

IA Labs. (2023). *How is AI Tech Like ChatGPT Improving Digital Accessibility?* IA Labs. https://ialabs.ie/how-is-ai-tech-like-chatgpt-improving-digital-accessibility/

IBM. (2023). *What is Machine Learning?* IBM. https://www.ibm.com/topics/machine-learning

Iheagwara, I. (2023). *6 Ways to Use ChatGPT as a Data Analyst.* Make Use Of. https://www.makeuseof.com/ways-to-use-chatgpt-data-analyst/

Ijari, K. (2023). *Design Principles For Conversational AI: A Primer.* Deepgram. https://deepgram.com/learn/design-principles-for-conversational-ai-a-primer

Ina. (2017). *The History of Chatbots - From ELIZA to Alexa.* Onlim. https://onlim.com/en/the-history-of-chatbots/

Indeed Editorial Team. (2021). *5 Ways To Improve Your Communication in Business and Why It's Important.* Indeed Career Guide. https://www.indeed.com/career-advice/career-development/importance-of-business-communication

Innodata. (2023). *How to Enhance ChatGPT with Prompt Engineering.* Innodata. https://innodata.com/how-to-enhance-chatgpt-with-prompt-engineering/

Instagantt. (2023). *What is ChatGPT and How Could You Use it for Project Management.* Instagantt. https://instagantt.com/project-management/how-to-use-chatgpt-for-project-management

InterviewBit. (2022). *Top 10 Characteristics of Artificial Intelligence.* InterviewBit. https://www.interviewbit.com/blog/characteristics-of-artificial-intelligence/

Inuwa, M. (2023). *An Introduction to Prompt Engineering.* Analytics Vidhya.

https://www.analyticsvidhya.com/blog/2023/06/what-is-prompt-engineering/

Israelsen, A. (2023). *How to Use ChatGPT to Write Code*. Plural Sight. https://www.pluralsight.com/blog/software-development/how-use-chatgpt-programming-coding

ITS Limited. (2017). *The Importance of Effective Communication in Business*. ITS Limited. https://www.itslimited.com/blog/news/the-importance-of-effective-communication-in-business/

Ivey, A. (2023). *How to Use ChatGPT to Learn a Language*. Cointelegraph. https://cointelegraph.com/news/how-to-use-chatgpt-to-learn-a-language

Ivey, A. (2023). *What is Prompt Engineering, and How Does it Work?* Cointelegraph. https://cointelegraph.com/news/what-is-prompt-engineering

Jain, T. (2023). *10 Best ChatGPT Prompts For Customer Service*. Enthu AI. https://enthu.ai/blog/chatgpt-prompts-for-customer-service/

Johnson, A. (2023). *How to Use ChatGPT and Bard for Everyday Tasks*. Forbes Australia. https://www.forbes.com.au/news/innovation/chatgpt-bard-use-everyday-tasks/

Kaikini, A. (2023). *9 Ways ChatGPT Can Make Your Life Easier*. Make Use Of. https://www.makeuseof.com/ways-chatgpt-can-make-life-easier/

Kan, M. (2023). *OpenAI: Sorry, ChatGPT Bug Leaked Payment Info to Other Users*. PC Mag. https://www.pcmag.com/news/openai-sorry-chatgpt-bug-leaked-payment-info-to-other-users#:~:text=AI-

Kapoor, M. (2023). *150 Best ChatGPT Prompts For Every Type Of Workflow*. GAiP. https://www.greataiprompts.com/chat-gpt/best-chat-gpt-prompts/

Kemper, J. (2023). *ChatGPT Guide: Use These Prompt Strategies to Maximize Your Results*. The Decoder. https://the-decoder.com/chatgpt-guide-prompt-strategies/#:~:text=ChatGPT%20does%20not%20need%20eloquent

Khoury, A. (2023). *Ways to Protect Your Privacy While Using ChatGPT and AI*. Komando. https://www.komando.com/security-privacy/chatgpt-privacy-issues/883444/

King, M. (2023). *How ChatGPT Can Help You To Learn Almost Any Foreign Language — From Zero to Hero!* Medium. https://medium.com/@neonforge/how-chatgpt-can-help-you-to-learn-almost-any-foreign-language-from-zero-to-hero-4d2ff7190cdc

Landwehr, J. (2023). *People Are Using ChatGPT in Place of Therapy—What Do*

Mental Health Experts Think? Health. https://www.health.com/chatgpt-therapy-mental-health-experts-weigh-in-7488513

Livevox. (2022). *5 AI Misconceptions, Debunked*. Livevox. https://livevox.com/5-ai-misconceptions-debunked/

Lim, C. K. (2019). *Singapore - Data Protection Overview*. Data Guidance. https://www.dataguidance.com/notes/singapore-data-protection-overview

Lutkevich, B. (2023). *What is GPT-4? Everything You Need to Know*. WhatIs; Tech Target. https://www.techtarget.com/whatis/definition/GPT-4

Luzia, R. (2023). *We Put Charisma Into Conversational AI*. VUI Agency. https://vui.agency/en/blog/chatgpt-the-redesign-of-conversation-design

Mack, L. (2023). *4 Ways to Use ChatGPT for Time Management*. Make Use Of. https://www.makeuseof.com/ways-to-use-chatgpt-time-management/

Macready, H. (2023). *65 ChatGPT Prompts for Marketing to Make Work Easier*. Hootsuite. https://blog.hootsuite.com/chatgpt-prompts-for-marketing/

Mailchimp. (2023). *Importance of Customer Service Explained: 8 Benefits*. Mailchimp. https://mailchimp.com/resources/importance-of-customer-service/#:

Marr, B. (2023). *10 Amazing Real-World Examples Of How Companies Are Using ChatGPT In 2023*. Forbes. https://www.forbes.com/sites/bernardmarr/2023/05/30/10-amazing-real-world-examples-of-how-companies-are-using-chatgpt-in-2023/?sh=27c4664f1441

Marr, B. (2023). *The Top 10 Limitations Of ChatGPT*. Forbes. https://www.forbes.com/sites/bernardmarr/2023/03/03/the-top-10-limitations-of-chatgpt/?sh=7314e2e08f35

Martinez, S. (2023). *How to Use ChatGPT as a Therapist*. GripRoom. https://www.griproom.com/fun/how-to-use-chatgpt-as-a-therapist#:

Maryville University. (2017). *The Top Trends Changing Marketing*. Maryville University. https://online.maryville.edu/blog/4-trends-changing-the-marketing-landscape/

Master Academia. (2023). *ChatGPT for Academics? Ethical Considerations of AI in Research*. Master Academia. https://master-academia.com/ethical-considerations-ai-research/

McCormick, K. (2023). *6 Ways to Use ChatGPT for Small Business Marketing (+6 Ways NOT to Use It)*. WordStream. https://www.wordstream.com/blog/ws/2023/03/06/how-to-use-chatgpt-for-small-business-marketing

McCoy, J. (2023). *ChatGPT for Content Creation: How to Write More in Less*

Time. Content at Scale. https://contentatscale.ai/blog/chatgpt-for-content-creation/

McKinsey & Company. (2022). *What is Innovation?* McKinsey & Company. https://www.mckinsey.com/featured-insights/mckinsey-explainers/what-is-innovation

McFadyen, R. (2023). *Importance of Quality Content Creation for Your Business.* Lead Genera. https://leadgenera.com/knowledge-hub/content-marketing/quality-content-creation-for-your-business/

McLean, D. (2023). *What is ChatGPT & 10 Creative Ways To Use It.* Elegant Themes. https://www.elegantthemes.com/blog/business/what-is-chatgpt

Miller, E. (2019). *10 Powerful Examples Of AI Applications In Today's World.* Magnimind Academy. https://magnimindacademy.com/blog/10-powerful-examples-of-ai-applications-in-todays-world/

Mitchell, C., Connolly, R., & Clarke, N. (2021). *How to Approach Conversation Design: The Basics (Part 1).* AWS Machine Learning. https://aws.amazon.com/blogs/machine-learning/part-1-approach-conversation-design-the-basics/

Mitchell, S. (2023). *How to Use ChatGPT to Develop Emotional Intelligence.* Make Use Of. https://www.makeuseof.com/use-chatgpt-develop-emotional-intelligence/

Moore, H. (2023). *ChatGPT Errors: How to Resolve Common Issues.* Cloud Booklet. https://www.cloudbooklet.com/chatgpt-errors/

Mottesi, C. (2023). *6 Uses of ChatGPT for Customer Service.* Invgate. https://blog.invgate.com/chatgpt-for-customer-service

Muñoz, E. (2021). *Attention is All You Need: Discovering the Transformer Paper.* Medium. https://towardsdatascience.com/attention-is-all-you-need-discovering-the-transformer-paper-73e5ff5e0634?gi=79094adf0d73

Murphy, T. (2023). *How to Use ChatGPT for Customer Service.* Tech Target. https://www.techtarget.com/searchcustomerexperience/feature/How-to-use-ChatGPT-for-customer-service

Mustufa, S. S. (2023). *ChatGPT and Data Privacy.* Tripwire. https://www.tripwire.com/state-of-security/chatgpt-and-data-privacy

Nagpal, M. (2023). *5 Interesting ChatGPT Applications and Examples.* Project Pro. https://www.projectpro.io/article/chatgpt-application-examples/713

Nerdy Nav. (2022). *73 Important ChatGPT Statistics & Facts For Mid Feb 2023 + An Infographic.* Nerdy Nav. https://nerdynav.com/chatgpt-statistics/

Neto, A. (2023). *How to Incorporate ChatGPT into Your Daily Routine.* LinkedIn.

https://www.linkedin.com/pulse/how-incorporate-chatgpt-your-daily-routine-aguimar-neto/

Nield, D. (2023a). *3 Ways to Prevent ChatGPT From Using You as Training Data*. Popular Science. https://www.popsci.com/diy/chatgpt-privacy-tips/

Nield, D. (2023b). *11 Tips to Take Your ChatGPT Prompts to the Next Level*. Wired. https://www.wired.com/story/11-tips-better-chatgpt-prompts/

Nova. (2023). *ChatGPT AI Chatbot*. Nova. https://novaapp.ai/blog/chatgpt-virtual-assistant

Oberoi, A. (2019). *The History and Evolution of Chatbots*. Daffodil. https://insights.daffodilsw.com/blog/the-history-and-evolution-of-chatbots

Ohio University. (2022). *Why is Data Analytics Important for Business?* Ohio University. https://www.ohio.edu/business/academics/graduate/online-masters-business-analytics/resources/data-analytics-businesses

OpenAI. (2023). *GPT-4 is OpenAI's Most Advanced System, Producing Safer and More Useful Responses*. OpenAI. https://openai.com/gpt-4

OpenAI. (2023). *New Ways to Manage Your Data in ChatGPT*. OpenAI. https://openai.com/blog/new-ways-to-manage-your-data-in-chatgpt

OpenAI. (2023). *Privacy Policy*. OpenAI. https://openai.com/policies/privacy-policy

Ortiz, S. (2023). *What is GPT-4? Here's Everything You Need to Know*. ZDNet. https://www.zdnet.com/article/what-is-gpt-4-heres-everything-you-need-to-know/

Owen, L. (2023). *Conversational design - Shaping the Future of UI*. Yellow. https://yellow.ai/blog/conversational-design/

Padmavati. (2023). *AI in Mental Health: ChatGPT's Role Explored*. Northwest Executive Education. https://northwest.education/?p=158981

Padmavati. (2023). *Master Business Communication with ChatGPT: A Guide*. Northwest Executive Education. https://northwest.education/insights/career-growth/mastering-business-communication-with-chatgpt/#:

Pai, A. (2023). *Analyzing Data Made Effortless Using ChatGPT*. Analytics Vidhya. https://www.analyticsvidhya.com/blog/2023/04/analyzing-data-using-chatgpt/

Patel, D. (2023). *GPT-4 Architecture, Infrastructure, Training Dataset, Costs, Vision, MoE*. Semi Analysis. https://www.semianalysis.com/p/gpt-4-architecture-infrastructure

Patterson, M. (2023). *Using ChatGPT for Customer Service*. Help Scout. https://www.helpscout.com/blog/chatgpt-customer-service/

Penn LPS. (2022). *5 Key Reasons Why Data Analytics is Important to Business*. Penn LPS Online. https://lpsonline.sas.upenn.edu/features/5-key-reasons-why-data-analytics-important-business

Perkel, J. M. (2023). *Six Tips for Better Coding with ChatGPT*. Nature, 618(7964), 422–423. https://doi.org/10.1038/d41586-023-01833-0

Petrosyan, V. (2023). *25 ChatGPT Examples For Digital Marketers & SEOs*. Search Engine Journal. https://www.searchenginejournal.com/chatgpt-examples/474937/

Pirnay, E. (2023). *We Spoke to People Who Started Using ChatGPT As Their Therapist*. Vice. https://www.vice.com/en/article/z3mnve/we-spoke-to-people-who-started-using-chatgpt-as-their-therapist

Plesea, A. (2022). *5 Benefits of AI-Powered Virtual Assistants Across the Retail Industry*. DruidAI. https://www.druidai.com/blog/5-benefits-of-ai-powered-virtual-assistants-across-the-retail-industry

Popova, A. (2023). *The Ultimate Localization Guide: Everything You Want to Know*. Redokun. https://redokun.com/blog/what-is-localization

Popovic, M. (2023). *ChatGPT Prompt Engineering: Techniques, Tips, and Applications*. Kanaries. https://docs.kanaries.net/articles/chatgpt-prompt-engineering

Potor, M. (2023). *What is Conversation Design?* Sinch Engage. https://engage.sinch.com/blog/what-is-conversation-design/

Press, G. (2016). *A Very Short History Of Artificial Intelligence (AI)*. Forbes. https://www.forbes.com/sites/gilpress/2016/12/30/a-very-short-history-of-artificial-intelligence-ai/?sh=ea226356fba2

Queensland Government. (2022). *Communicating Effectively*. Queensland Government. https://www.business.qld.gov.au/running-business/marketing-sales/sales/communicating-effectively#:

Quote Investigator. (2014). *The Biggest Problem in Communication Is the Illusion That It Has Taken Place*. Quote Investigator. https://quoteinvestigator.com/2014/08/31/illusion/

Rahaman, M. (2023). *Digital Marketing in the Era of AI*. LinkedIn. https://www.linkedin.com/pulse/digital-marketing-era-ai-artificial-intelligence-mizanur-rahaman/

Ramos, C. (2023). *Learn How to Use the ChatGPT Chatbot With Virtual Assistants*. Outsourcing Angel. https://outsourcingangel.com/how-to-use-chatgpt-with-virtual-assistants/

Rampton, J. (2023). *The Advantages and Disadvantages of ChatGPT*. Calendar.

https://www.calendar.com/blog/the-advantages-and-disadvantages-of-chatgpt/

Reyes, D. (2023). *New ChatGPT-4 Strengths, Weaknesses, and Limitations.* The Good Vibes Corner. https://medium.com/the-good-vibes-corner/new-chatgpt-4-strengths-weaknesses-and-limitations-86834e2dd6ba

Riserbato, R. (2021). *7 Benefits of Consistent, High-Quality Content Marketing.* Hubspot. https://blog.hubspot.com/marketing/benefits-high-quality-content-consistency-brand

Sakamoto, A. (2023). *GPT-4 is Out And What Does it Mean for Chat GPT Data Analytics.* Kanaries. https://docs.kanaries.net/articles/chatgpt-4-data-analytics

Santiago, E. (2023). *190 ChatGPT Prompts Marketers Should Use.* Hubspot. https://blog.hubspot.com/marketing/chatgpt-prompts

Sarkis, L. (2023). *The Emotional Potential of ChatGPT: 5 Innovative Use Cases.* LinkedIn. https://www.linkedin.com/pulse/emotional-potential-chatgpt-5-innovative-use-cases-louis-sarkis/

Sharabi, C. (2023). *How OpenAI and ChatGPT Will Impact Localization.* Blend. https://www.getblend.com/blog/how-openai-and-chatgpt-will-impact-localization/

Shiksha Online. (2023). *How ChatGPT is Used for Data Analytics?* Shiksha Online. https://www.shiksha.com/online-courses/articles/10-exciting-applications-of-chat-gpt-for-data-analysis/

Shukuya, M. (2023). *Turn ChatGPT Into Your Personal Assistant With These Useful Prompts.* Cheapism. https://blog.cheapism.com/awesome-chatgpt-prompts/

Simon, E. (2023). *6 Ways to Use ChatGPT to Learn a Foreign Language.* International Center for Language Studies. https://www.icls.edu/6-ways-to-use-chatgpt-to-learn-a-foreign-language/

Simpson, A. (2023). *9 ChatGPT Success Stories to Highlight What You Can Do in 2023.* Niche Pursuits. https://www.nichepursuits.com/chatgpt-success-stories/

Singh, I. (2023). *Say Goodbye to Siri: How to Use ChatGPT as a Virtual Assistant.* LinkedIn. https://www.linkedin.com/pulse/say-goodbye-siri-how-use-chatgpt-virtual-assistant-inderjeet-singh/

Singh, V. (2023). *How Virtual Assistants in ChatGPT?* Medium. https://medium.com/@varunsnghsuperdude/how-virtual-assistants-in-chatgpt-56fa06b5b4ef

Smarty, A. (2023). *ChatGPT Prompts for Customer Support*. Practical Ecommerce. https://www.practicalecommerce.com/chatgpt-prompts-for-customer-support

Smulders, S. (2023). *15 Rules For Crafting Effective GPT Chat Prompts*. Expandi. https://expandi.io/blog/chat-gpt-rules/

Solis, T. (2023). *9 Ways to Use ChatGPT for Language Learning*. Scribbr. https://www.scribbr.com/ai-tools/CHATGPT-language-learning/

Sorkin, D. H., Janio, E. A., Eikey, E. V., Schneider, M., Davis, K., Schueller, S. M., Stadnick, N. A., Zheng, K., Neary, M., Safani, D., & Mukamel, D. B. (2021). *Rise in Use of Digital Mental Health Tools and Technologies in the United States During the COVID-19 Pandemic: Survey Study*. Journal of Medical Internet Research, 23(4). https://doi.org/10.2196/26994

Souza, M. (2023). *The Rise of Conversational AI and Its Impact on UX Design*. LinkedIn. https://www.linkedin.com/pulse/rise-conversational-ai-its-impact-ux-design-marcela-souza/

Stefanski, R. (2022). *8 Ways AI Will Change the Future of Marketing*. Engati. https://www.engati.com/blog/8-ways-ai-will-change-the-future-of-marketing

Stitch Resource. (2023). *5 Benefits of Data Analytics for Your Business*. Stitch Resource. https://www.stitchdata.com/resources/benefits-of-data-analytics/

Success Team. (2022). *What Is OpenAI?* Speak AI. https://speakai.co/what-is-openai/

Supply Chain Today. (2022). *The Best ChatGPT Quotes*. Supply Chain Today. https://www.supplychaintoday.com/best-chatgpt-quotes/

Surveypal. (2023). *How to Use ChatGPT to Improve Customer Service*. LinkedIn. https://www.linkedin.com/pulse/how-use-chatgpt-improve-customer-service-surveypal/

Sypnotix. (2023). *10 Ways I Use ChatGPT At Home and Work*. Sypnotix. https://www.sypnotix.com/reviews/10-ways-i-use-chatgpt-at-home-and-work

Tableau. (2023). *What is the History of Artificial Intelligence (AI)?* Tableau. https://www.tableau.com/data-insights/ai/history#:

The Decision Lab. (2023). *Google Effect*. The Decision Lab. https://thedecisionlab.com/biases/google-effect

Timothy, M. (2023). *7 Ways to Get the Best Results From ChatGPT*. Make Use Of. https://www.makeuseof.com/how-to-get-best-results-from-chatgpt/

Toppr. (2019). *History of Computers: Parts, Networking, Operating Systems, FAQs*.

230 References

Toppr. https://www.toppr.com/guides/computer-aptitude-and-knowledge/basics-of-computers/history-of-computers/#:

Trombetti, M. (2023). *Discover How ChatGPT and LLMs will Rewrite the Language Industry.* Translated. https://translated.com/chatgpt-in-localization

Truly, A. (2022). *5 Amazing Things People Have Done With ChatGPT.* Digital Trends. https://www.digitaltrends.com/computing/5-amazing-things-with-chatgpt/

Tsuei, J. (2023). *Use ChatGPT for Time Management.* Clockwise. https://www.getclockwise.com/blog/chatgpt-time-management#:

Unguess. (2023). *The Role of AI in Improving Digital Accessibility.* Unguess. https://blog.unguess.io/ai-improving-digital-accessibility

Uzialko, A. (2023). *How Artificial Intelligence Is Transforming Business.* Business News Daily. https://www.businessnewsdaily.com/9402-artificial-intelligence-business-trends.html

Vasylkiv, B. (2023). *Limitations and Ethical Considerations of Using ChatGPT.* Incora. https://incora.software/insights/chatgpt-limitations

Veale, K. (2023). *Does ChatGPT Have Privacy Issues?* Make Use Of. https://www.makeuseof.com/chatgpt-privacy-issues/

Verma, P. (2023). *What to Know About OpenAI, the Company Behind ChatGPT.* Washington Post. https://www.washingtonpost.com/technology/2023/02/06/what-is-openai-chatgpt/

Wade, T. (2023). *100+ ChatGPT Prompts for Creators: Speed Up Your Workflow With AI.* Descript. https://www.descript.com/blog/article/100-chatgpt-prompts-for-creators-speed-up-your-workflow-with-ai

Wagh, A. (2023). *What's New in GPT-4: An Overview of the GPT-4 Architecture and Capabilities of Next-Generation AI.* Medium. https://medium.com/@amol-wagh/whats-new-in-gpt-4-an-overview-of-the-gpt-4-architecture-and-capabilities-of-next-generation-ai-900c445d5ffe

Wake Forest. (2015). *5 Challenges of Mental Health Care Today.* WFU Online Counseling. https://counseling.online.wfu.edu/blog/5-challenges-of-mental-health-care-today/

WeConnect. (2023). *How Digital Solutions are Revolutionizing Mental Health Support.* WeConnect. https://www.weconnecthealth.io/blog/how-digital-solutions-are-revolutionizing-mental-health-support

White, M. (2022). *Top 10 Most Insane Things ChatGPT Has Done This Week.*

Springboard Blog. https://www.springboard.com/blog/news/chatgpt-revolution/

Woods, R. (2023). *AI + you: How to Use ChatGPT for Content Creation.* Microsoft Create. https://create.microsoft.com/en-us/learn/articles/how-to-use-chatgpt-for-content-creation

Wu, G. (2022). *8 Big Problems With OpenAI's ChatGPT.* Make Use Of. https://www.makeuseof.com/openai-chatgpt-biggest-probelms/

Xiong, G. (2022). *Why It's Important to Care for Your Mental Health.* Doctor on Demand. https://doctorondemand.com/blog/mental-health/why-its-important-to-care-for-your-mental-health/

Yalalov, D. (2023). *Prompt Engineering Ultimate Guide 2023: Beginner to Advanced.* Metaverse Post. https://mpost.io/prompt-engineering-ultimate-guide/

Yohai. (2023). *ChatGPT Prompts for Health - ChatGPT 4.* ChatGPT4. https://chatgpt4.uk/chatgpt-prompts-for-health/

Zabój, D. (2020). *8 Principles of Conversation Design for Making Better Chatbot Conversations.* ChatBot. https://www.chatbot.com/blog/conversational-design/

Zahoor, A. (2023). *9 Ways To Use ChatGPT For Content Creation.* Hacker Noon. https://hackernoon.com/9-ways-to-use-chatgpt-for-content-creation

Zakaryan, V. (2023). *What are Common Misconceptions About AI?* PostIndustria. https://postindustria.com/what-are-common-misconceptions-about-ai-machine-learning/

Zimmerman, S. (2022). *AI and Localization: The New Way Forward.* Summa Linguae. https://summalinguae.com/localization/ai-and-localization/

Printed in Great Britain
by Amazon